Yours Truly, John:

Seven Signs of the Messiah

A Scripture Reflection Guide

Traci Stead

TABLE OF CONTENTS

INTRODUCTION

I have a box of love letters and cards hidden away in a secret spot. Occasionally I open the box and leaf through the yellowing papers that reveal a love song of passionate promises offered by a young man who loved me, who wanted to call me his own.

Another box, not so hidden, lies beneath my bedside table. In it are more letters and cards that speak of mature love, of gratitude and deep desire that come only through age and experience. Poetry and prose that come from time together, a life lived in love.

Someday, I imagine, my grandchildren will discover the boxes and ask me about them. I'll tell them of a young man, his eyes shining and cheeks pink with excitement, who sat across from me dumbstruck and speechless. I'll tell them of a love that lasted years and years, like a fire growing hotter the longer it burned.

This is the Gospel of John. It's a book of stories describing John's love for the Messiah, Jesus the Christ. It was written toward the end of his life, when the love had grown beyond infatuation and reckless folly. It is a love story of depth and devotion.

And I envision it as a telling to the next generation. The children have come to listen to the stories of old Uncle John. It's a weekend reunion, and perhaps the last time the family will gather while Uncle John is still able to be with them, still able to share the family stories that make them who they are.

This scripture reflection guide is not your regular Bible study. I've tried to connect the ancient bones of the characters with new tendons and muscles, filling out the skeleton with some flesh and blood. Tears have traced new paths down the dry, dusty cheeks of those who encountered Christ. And new blood has pumped through the hearts of those who loved him.

The stories are born from characters in John's gospel. I have read and reread the stories until I feel like I am sitting around the campfire too. The stories are my imaginings, of how it may have happened, but the lives are real, the love palpable.

Each chapter includes a fictional telling of how the story might have sounded with more detail than John offers. I call this "A Reunion." The characters in John's story are seldom named. I have taken the liberty to name them, describe them, and give them life. It is important for you to understand that the first section of each chapter is how I imagine it might have been. You may have your own ideas, as you should; no one experiences a story exactly as the next person.

After the fictional account of the story, you are asked to read a section of John from the Bible. This is "An Ancient Story." I will often ask you to look for or focus on words or phrases as you read. These are intended to keep your mind on the reading, to help you listen to what God may have to say to you personally. I have included the scriptures within the book so you don't lose focus by going between this book and a copy of the Bible.

However, if you prefer a version other than the English Standard Version, then please bring it along.

The third section in each chapter is "A Modern Story." It's a true modern account of a similar event. John writes his book showing us that Jesus is involved in the lives around him. He cares. He loves. He works. I'm writing to show that Jesus is the same now and forever. He still cares, still loves, still works.

The fourth section is "Reflection." Now that you've seen the story in three ways, how does it affect you? How do you see Jesus caring, loving, and working in your own life?

Finally, love is active. It pursues the object of its desire. An author always hopes to write something that will change lives, to somehow make a difference. I believe John did just that. So the fifth section is "Action." I ask you to do something about the story. I want you to get out there and spread the message that Jesus is the Messiah.

You may choose to complete this study on your own, but I encourage you to meet with family and/or friends to discuss what you are learning. You can read each section in ten to twenty minutes. How much time you spend in actual reflection and action is up to you. If you choose to complete it in a weekly group setting, it should take nine weeks. Be sure to set aside time for the "Action" activities.

Thank you for taking this journey with me!

CHAPTER 1

HE COMES

✤ A REUNION ✤

"Stop pushing," whined Caleb, elbowing his brother as he scooted a little closer to the fire.

The children were gathered two rows deep in front of the older family members and friends. The large fire cast shadows across the diverse group on the sandy beach of the Great Sea. Benches were lined with the elderly and a few expectant mothers with swollen bellies. Men stood in the back. The leader rose as a hush fell over the crowd.

"In the beginning all was darkness."

The children followed the graceful curve of the man's hand as he traced the expanse of darkness outside the campfire circle.

"Let there be light," the leader commanded, his voice deep and husky.

As if on cue, a log fell over and a spray of sparks flashed into the darkness. The younger children startled and then giggled.

"God saw that the light was good, and he separated the light from the darkness. He called the light *day*, and the darkness *night*, and the first day was done." The leader slowly bowed low, curving his back and drawing in his arms. Quickly he unrolled his large frame and threw his arms heavenward. "Then God separated the mighty waters with a great expanse that he named *sky*. And there was evening and morning. The second day was done."

The children sat at attention, some with legs crisscrossed, others up on their knees. Their parents had talked of nothing else for weeks. This great gathering of friends and loved ones was a special reunion to celebrate the return of their old friend, John.

Now the leader was scooping a shallow furrow in the sand with his large hands. From behind his back he produced a pitcher and began pouring water into the trough.

"Let the water be gathered to one place and let the dry ground appear," he said as the water filled the trench. "God called the dry ground *land*, and the waters he called *seas*, and he saw that it was good."

"I came here on the sea," piped Caleb.

The older children and adults shushed him, but the storyteller only smiled and nodded.

"Let the land produce plants and trees, fruits and vegetables." He pulled tiny wildflowers from his robe and handed them to the youngest children. "And let each one produce seeds to bear more of its own kind. It was so, and the sun set on the third day. Then God saw that the heavens were empty and dark, so he filled them with stars and planets. He made the sun to warm us by day, and the moon to strengthen us at night."

The storyteller pointed to the bright moon overhead. Everyone looked up.

"God saw that it was good, and the fourth day was done."

The leader stepped on an upturned log, and the children watched, wide-eyed.

"On the fifth day God fashioned the birds that fly in the sky. He made the little songbirds: the turtledove, swallow, and cuckoo. He made the birds of prey: the falcon and owl. God even made the loud, raucous birds, like raven and crow."

The men on the back row burst into cackles and caws. Everybody laughed and added their own birdcalls.

"God made the birds of the sea: the pelicans, cormorants, and ospreys." The leader called above the racket as he waved his long arms up and down like wings. "And then he made the sea creatures that swarm in the waters of the earth: great sea monsters and fish and eels."

The crowd quieted.

"Morning and evening came and went, and the fifth day was done."

"Now come the animals," Caleb half whispered to his brother, Paul.

"Then God made the livestock," the leader said as an older boy handed him a young goat. He stroked the kid while it lay in his arms. "He made goats and sheep, cattle and donkeys, horses and oxen. He made the small creatures that move along the ground: the snakes and salamanders, the frogs and the newts. Then he made the wild animals that hunt and prowl: the bear and coyote, the lion and fox."

The storyteller handed the goat back to the boy and slowly turned on his heels, sinking down to the sand like a limp rag tossed on the table. The children twisted to see what he might do now, but he lay quiet and still.

An old man rose and walked to where the storyteller stood. The man's stooped shoulders gave away his age and the pain that his life now held. He knelt beside the storyteller and scooped some sand into his hands. He lifted the sand above his head.

His voice, low and quiet, beat a rhythm like night waves on the side of a boat. "Then God said, 'Let us make man in our image.' The Lord God formed the man." The old gentleman let the sand sift between his fingers and fall onto the storyteller's chest. "And he breathed into the man the breath of life, and the man became a living being."

At that the storyteller inhaled deeply and lifted himself in one fluid movement from the sand. Together the two men said, "The sixth day was done."

"I don't want to go to bed yet," Caleb pleaded, knowing that the story always ended with the seventh day of rest.

"Tonight you stay for the rest of the stories." The storyteller smiled as he chucked Caleb under the chin.

Caleb glanced back at his mother and saw her smile and nod. *Yes*, she mouthed. His face brightened, and he turned back toward the fire.

The spry storyteller helped the old man to his feet.

"Darkness reigned in the Time Before," the old man began. "God looked upon the darkness and had an idea. He spotted in the back of his mind a twinkle, a little speck of light glowing at the end of a kindling stick. He pulled it forth and waved it round and round until the light took shape at the command of his voice. The Word was with God because the Word was God. Though the Word was new, the Word had always been. The Word spoke and all that is, or ever was, drew breath because of the Word. The Word was bright and shone its light into the darkness. The darkness retreated and was not able to overcome the light, nor will it ever." His voice rose in a crescendo.

"Amen," called a man in the back.

Caleb turned to see who had spoken. The campfire glanced off the faces in the circle. His mother shifted uncomfortably on the bench with the other swollen mothers. His father stood in the back, a large man fully five inches above everyone else in the gathering. He flicked his fingers at Caleb and the boy quickly faced the storyteller.

"A smaller light than the Word shone in the darkness, leading us to him, like a single candle lighting the dark alleys of the city. Shadows played on the walls and grabbed at our cloaks, but the candle walked toward the Word and the light grew around us.

"The breath that spoke light into being was the very light itself. That light came into the world, and though the world had been created by the light, it could not see by the light. The world continued to hide in the dark." Remorse echoed in his voice, making the women tear up.

"I'm afraid of the dark," Caleb whispered to the night.

"We aren't in the dark," Paul answered back. "It's safe here."

"The candle shone on the dank, mold-covered alleyways until the darkness called out to it. 'Where are you from?' it asked. But the candle only walked toward the light of the Word."

"How can a candle walk?" Caleb asked. His eyebrows furrowed in confusion.

The old man laughed out loud, and everyone joined in.

"The candle was a person," the old man said. "His name was John, and he had come into the world to shine a light on our dark path. He showed us Jesus, the living Word of God."

"Oh." Caleb hunched his shoulders and looked down, embarrassed.

Paul pointed at him and laughed, but the old man stooped in front of Caleb and held his small, chubby hand.

"I'm sorry. What's your name?" the old man asked.

"Caleb," the little boy mumbled. Shame swam at the edge of his brown eyes.

"Caleb, my name is John—a different John than in the tale I'm telling now. You came from far away to hear my stories. I'm sorry for being too hard to understand. Will you listen longer if I speak more plainly?" He smiled at the boy.

Caleb nodded his head and wiped the tears with the back of his hand.

✠ An Ancient Story ✠
(John 1)

John was written around 90 AD to a diverse group of Christians. Some were Jewish; they knew the stories and had ideas about God, prophets, and the chosen race. Some were Gentiles; they had heard of the God of the Jews, but now they accepted him as their God too.

As you read the first chapter of John in the pages that follow, notice the similarities in John to the creation story in Genesis. The other gospel writers start their stories at the beginning of Jesus's life or ministry, but John goes all the way back to the beginning of creation. Notice, too, the ways John extends that story to include the Gentiles. John begins his book with poetry, much like the book of Genesis begins. He says that Jesus was with God as Word, life, and light.

1. How would you poetically describe Jesus?

We don't know if John ever married, but I'm sure he was a romantic. Any woman would have swooned to read his love letters. He used symbolism, poetry, and prose to create a masterful story. Just look at his beginning.

Chapter 1 covers six days: five actual days, the last day being three days after the fourth. On the first day John the Baptist declared he was not the Messiah. On the second day John declared that Jesus was the Chosen One and baptized Jesus. The third day Jesus began calling his disciples, and on the fourth day Philip and Nathanael joined them. Nathanael agreed that Jesus was the Messiah. Chapter 2 begins three days later at a wedding. It was on this, the seventh day, that Jesus completed his first miracle and the disciples put their faith in him. Like the story of creation, all was now complete.

2. What words stand out to you as you read? How do you picture each scene in John 1?

In the accounts of Matthew, Mark, and Luke, Jesus told everyone to keep his identity a secret. He asked the people not to talk about his miracles but to give glory to God. He commanded the demons to be quiet when they shouted his name. But John's gospel is different. He wanted his readers to know who Jesus was (and is). In fact, as John neared the end of his book, he wrote that "Jesus performed many other signs in the presence of his disciples, which are not recorded in this book. But these are written that you may believe that Jesus is the Messiah, the Son of God, and that by believing you may have life in his name" (John 20:30-31 NIV).

When we look back at John's prologue, it's easy to see why John the Baptist was called a witness to the light and not the actual light. In 1:19-28, John declared that he was not the Messiah or the Prophet, but rather a voice calling in the wilderness. This was a reference to Isaiah's prophecy in the Old Testament (Isaiah 40:3).

In 1:29-34, John the Baptist described in detail how Jesus was the Lamb of God, that although Jesus was younger than John, Jesus came first. John related that the Spirit of God rested on Jesus, and finally John called Jesus *God's Chosen One*.

But this declaration was not John the Baptist's alone. He was joined by the disciples. First, Andrew told his brother, Simon Peter, that they had found the Messiah. Then when Nathanael joined the group, Jesus declared him a true Israelite in whom there was no deceit. Their conversation continued with Nathanael's declaration that Jesus was the Son of God and the King of Israel.

3. **What title would you give Jesus?**

Often the journey to Jesus begins with doubts and uncertainties. Perhaps you have heard stories. You've seen others' faith. You may have even tried reading the Bible and praying, but you just aren't sure that Jesus is who he said.

Don't worry, you're in good company. Does it surprise you that the one who was sent to prepare the way for the Messiah didn't even recognize him at first?

4. **What was the sign for John that Jesus was the Messiah?**

5. **If you are a believer, what word first shined light and life into your heart? How do you know who Jesus is?**

JOHN 1

[1] In the beginning was the Word, and the Word was with God, and the Word was God. [2] He was in the beginning with God. [3] All things were made through him, and without him was not any thing made that was made. [4] In him was life, and the life was the light of men. [5] The light shines in the darkness, and the darkness has not overcome it.

[6] There was a man sent from God, whose name was John. [7] He came as a witness, to bear witness about the light, that all might believe through him. [8] He was not the light, but came to bear witness about the light.

[9] The true light, which gives light to everyone, was coming into the world. [10] He was in the world, and the world was made through him, yet the world did not know him. [11] He came to his own, and his own people did not receive him. [12] But to all who did receive him, who believed in his name, he gave the right to become children of God, [13] who were born, not of blood nor of the will of the flesh nor of the will of man, but of God.

[14] And the Word became flesh and dwelt among us, and we have seen his glory, glory as of the only Son from the Father, full of grace and truth. [15] (John bore witness about him, and cried out, "This was he of whom I said, 'He who comes after me ranks before me, because he was before me.'") [16] For from his fullness we have all received, grace upon grace. [17] For the law was given through Moses; grace and truth came through Jesus Christ. [18] No one has

ever seen God; the only God, who is at the Father's side, he has made him known.

¹⁹ And this is the testimony of John, when the Jews sent priests and Levites from Jerusalem to ask him, "Who are you?" ²⁰ He confessed, and did not deny, but confessed, "I am not the Christ." ²¹ And they asked him, "What then? Are you Elijah?" He said, "I am not." "Are you the Prophet?" And he answered, "No." ²² So they said to him, "Who are you? We need to give an answer to those who sent us. What do you say about yourself?" ²³ He said, "I am the voice of one crying out in the wilderness, 'Make straight the way of the Lord,' as the prophet Isaiah said."

²⁴ (Now they had been sent from the Pharisees.) ²⁵ They asked him, "Then why are you baptizing, if you are neither the Christ, nor Elijah, nor the Prophet?" ²⁶ John answered them, "I baptize with water, but among you stands one you do not know, ²⁷ even he who comes after me, the strap of whose sandal I am not worthy to untie." ²⁸ These things took place in Bethany across the Jordan, where John was baptizing.

²⁹ The next day he saw Jesus coming toward him, and said, "Behold, the Lamb of God, who takes away the sin of the world! ³⁰ This is he of whom I said, 'After me comes a man who ranks before me, because he was before me.' ³¹ I myself did not know him, but for this purpose I came baptizing with water, that he might be revealed to Israel." ³² And John bore witness: "I saw the Spirit descend from heaven like a dove, and it remained on him. ³³ I myself did not know him, but he who sent me to baptize with water said to me, 'He on whom you see the Spirit descend

and remain, this is he who baptizes with the Holy Spirit.' ³⁴ And I have seen and have borne witness that this is the Son of God."

³⁵ The next day again John was standing with two of his disciples, ³⁶ and he looked at Jesus as he walked by and said, "Behold, the Lamb of God!" ³⁷ The two disciples heard him say this, and they followed Jesus. ³⁸ Jesus turned and saw them following and said to them, "What are you seeking?" And they said to him, "Rabbi" (which means Teacher), "where are you staying?" ³⁹ He said to them, "Come and you will see." So they came and saw where he was staying, and they stayed with him that day, for it was about the tenth hour. ⁴⁰ One of the two who heard John speak and followed Jesus was Andrew, Simon Peter's brother. ⁴¹ He first found his own brother Simon and said to him, "We have found the Messiah" (which means Christ). ⁴² He brought him to Jesus. Jesus looked at him and said, "You are Simon the son of John. You shall be called Cephas" (which means Peter).

⁴³ The next day Jesus decided to go to Galilee. He found Philip and said to him, "Follow me." ⁴⁴ Now Philip was from Bethsaida, the city of Andrew and Peter. ⁴⁵ Philip found Nathanael and said to him, "We have found him of whom Moses in the Law and also the prophets wrote, Jesus of Nazareth, the son of Joseph." ⁴⁶ Nathanael said to him, "Can anything good come out of Nazareth?" Philip said to him, "Come and see." ⁴⁷ Jesus saw Nathanael coming toward him and said of him, "Behold, an Israelite indeed, in whom there is no deceit!" ⁴⁸ Nathanael said to him, "How do you know me?" Jesus answered him,

"Before Philip called you, when you were under the fig tree, I saw you." [49] Nathanael answered him, "Rabbi, you are the Son of God! You are the King of Israel!" [50] Jesus answered him, "Because I said to you, 'I saw you under the fig tree,' do you believe? You will see greater things than these." [51] And he said to him, "Truly, truly, I say to you, you will see heaven opened, and the angels of God ascending and descending on the Son of Man."

✛ A MODERN STORY ✛

Invisible darkness slithered over the hot desert. A quiet wind whispered through the date palms lining the palace walls. It was July 1979, and Saddam Hussein was taking power in Iraq. It was a very public purge as members of Parliament were forced from the room to be tortured and executed. In just a few short months hundreds of powerful people were arrested or killed. Less than a year later Hussein began a war against Iran that resulted in the deaths of a million people.

The same year that this deep darkness descended into the desert, a child was born. His name was Wissam. He was born in Baghdad, and his childhood was spent dodging bombs and bullets. Wissam and his friends played in bombed-out craters, shooting pretend guns and throwing rock grenades. Children, after all, always imitate what they see.

When the war against Iran ended, Iraq faced severe sanctions for thirteen years. Hussein tried to unite the people himself but was unsuccessful, so he tried to bring them together through religion. By making Islam state-sanctioned and state-mandated, he created a rules-based religion that offered no hope.

Because of the sanctions Iraqis had little food and little water. Wissam's family lived on one dollar a month. But more than physical food and water, they starved and thirsted for hope.

When Wissam was seventeen, his four-year-old sister died of something as simple as food poisoning. Medical help and supplies were for the wealthy. His mother looked to the Quran for hope but found none. She was told only that her little girl would be judged for her guilt.

A few months later Wissam's uncle died of cancer. He had lived in obedience to the Quran his entire life, but once he became ill, he couldn't complete the purification rites. He died hopeless, condemned by Islam to hell.

Wissam lost all faith. He secretly renounced Islam. He continued attending Friday prayers and participating in the fasting and feasting of Ramadan so that he wouldn't attract attention. Fear did nothing to brighten his darkness. Finally he completely rejected any belief in God.

The darkness chased Wissam through days, weeks, and years as he continued to run from religion. He became intrigued with all things American. He listened to the Voice of America radio station. He read American stories, watched American movies. And he wondered, *What are these strange scriptures that are quoted?* He was surprised to even hear the Bible quoted in the 1996 movie *Mission: Impossible*—"... kings and rulers of the earth, who built for themselves places now lying in ruins ..." (Job 3:14 NIV).

Wissam had been taught that the Bible was correct, as long as it agreed with the Quran. The sacred texts of the Bible had come first, he knew, but he'd been told it sometimes disagreed with the Quran. Islam taught that these disagreements were places that Christians and Jews had twisted the holy scriptures.

One day, as Wissam weaved through the narrow booths and colorful tents of a local flea market, he stopped to pick up a book. It was an Arabic copy of the Gospel of John. He glanced sideways, peering around the crowded streets. He reached into his pocket, pulled out a handful of coins, and spent his precious money to buy what he thought was the Bible.

He hurried home and hid himself away in his room. He read the book like a treasure hunter, looking for the quotes he had read in other books and heard in movies. They weren't there. *Everyone is right. The Bible must be messed up. It's no better than the Quran.* He stared at his reflection in the night window.

But he couldn't get the rebel Jesus out of his mind. Here was a guy who did the things Wissam wanted to do. He exposed the hypocrisy of the religious authorities. Instead of condemnation, he offered hope and love.

Wissam returned to the flea market, and there he discovered another book, a thicker book. He spent the last of his money to buy the faded and tattered volume. It took longer to read, but Wissam now knew that the Gospel of John was not itself the Bible. He had found a New Testament, of which John was just a part. A match was struck in the darkness.

Yet this book seemed to only be part of a larger book as well. There were references to other scriptures, to other stories. This time Wissam knew he didn't have a complete Bible. He needed to read the rest of the story to see if what he had been taught was correct.

But he was out of money.

He borrowed some funds from his cousin and headed back to the flea market. Among the dusty copies of cast-aside books, he found an entire Bible. He took it home and read it from cover to cover. *The author of this book really knows his stuff,* he mused. The Bible's history and geography were exactly what Wissam had been taught and could even see for himself.

One day at the college he was attending, Wissam noticed a man praying and crossing himself. He stopped to ask the man if what he had read in the Bible was true. "Yes," the student said, and then he began to teach Wissam about Jesus.

A yellow glow flickered on the horizon.

But like a birthday candle, Wissam's hope was blown to smoke when his mother found the Bibles stashed away in his room.

"You bring shame and disgrace to our family with these blasphemous books." Tears traced her cheeks and fear flashed in her eyes. She shook him by the shirt collar. "Get rid of those books."

Wissam obeyed.

But even after disposing of the books, he couldn't rid himself of the stories he'd read. His mind continued to fan the smoldering coals. He bought another Bible, this time in English, and hid it away, reading in secret.

In 2000, Wissam finished college with an engineering degree, and in 2001, he completed his military duty. He found a job working as a sanitary engineer and began saving his money.

In October 2009, thirty years after Saddam Hussein brought terror and darkness to Iraq, Wissam was walking down the staircase of his office building when a car bomb exploded outside. Around 1,500 people in the area were either killed or injured. Wissam never suffered a scratch. He believed there was a reason.

Wissam was by now reading his Bible daily. At a local internet café his earbuds secretly played Christian music, and he began taking an online Bible course. The woman who graded his online tests asked if he had any prayer requests. Did he ever.

"Please pray that I can be baptized and can live in a place where I am free to be a Christian." It was the same prayer he had been praying for years.

Wissam became connected with a British believer who stressed baptism for the forgiveness of sins. Wissam asked the man what he should do since he knew of no one there who could baptize him. The man bought a ticket for Wissam to travel to northern Iraq, where they could meet. Wissam was baptized in a hotel bathtub, raised to life in a bright, shining world that didn't recognize him.

That was May 26, 2010. Just a few days later the first Iraqi visitor visas to America were approved. Wissam received one of them, told his family good-bye, and boarded a plane for America with a few dollars and one bag of clothing. He had no idea what was about to happen.

In America he traveled to the home of the woman who had graded his Bible correspondence course. He stayed with her in rural Pennsylvania and filed an application for religious asylum. Within the year he was connected to churches, attending a school to study the Bible, and holding a hope for the future.

But darkness still lurked at the edges of Wissam's world. He knew that light and hope were withheld from the world's Muslim population, from the people he knew and loved. He wanted to show them the light.

Now Wissam ministers to the largest Muslim population in the United States. He brings light and hope to the darkness of

Detroit. He has gone to those who are his own in hopes that they will not reject the one who came so long ago.[1]

✛ REFLECTION ✛

I sat in a stubby meadow overlooking the autumn hillside. Edges of green leaves were beginning to tinge in a gold-and-red haze. The hard tips of mowed grass poked through my jeans and made my legs itch. I was eighteen. The rolling hills below me echoed a new song. I had lived there all my life; they were familiar and common. Yet they were strangely new.

I had moved away from home and was working as a nanny in a local university town. The six-year-old child I cared for was profoundly disabled, suffering seizures daily, unable to communicate. I wanted to do something to help, but what could I do?

It was the first time I remember listening for God. I had prayed, many times in fact. In my mind, prayer was telling God what was bothering me and asking him to fix it. This was different. This time I didn't ask for anything. I just waited and listened.

That day—staring across the expanse of trees, mountains, and crisp blue sky—was the beginning. It is what I mark as the start of my growth as a Christian. I had been baptized before. I had worshipped every Sunday my entire life. It wasn't the beginning

---

1   This section is based on material from the following sources:
    Bobby Ross Jr., "The Long Road from Baghdad," The Christian Chronicle, Sept. 21, 2015, accessed March 2017, christianchronicle.org/the-long-road-from-baghdad/.
    "Understanding Islam and Reaching Muslims," Waterford Church of Christ, Oct. 20, 2013, accessed March 2017, waterfordcoc.org/understanding-islam.

of knowledge, but the beginning of a mutual relationship, one in which I would serve and not just be served.

John began his gospel at the very beginning, at the creation of the world. For John it secured the power and authority of God and of Jesus who was with him.

John was most likely writing to second-generation Christians. They were Jews who believed in Jesus Christ as the Messiah, and they were Gentiles who had joined the kingdom of God. Both groups needed reassurance that what they had been taught was truth.

At that point it was about sixty years after Jesus's ascension. Very few were left who had seen Jesus. These followers were those whom Jesus spoke of when he said, "... blessed are those who have not seen and yet have believed" (John 20:29 NIV).

Like Wissam they had heard whispers that darkened the doorway to God. John told his audience that the light shines in the darkness, and the darkness is driven out. Perhaps John's audience was also feeling driven out as persecutions across the Roman Empire increased. They were afraid. They were hiding. Their lights were flickering.

John reassured his people that many did not recognize Jesus when he came, but to those who did pay attention, he offered hope. He gave grace and truth.

As John moved past the beginning, he portrayed a Messiah who desires more than service. He wants relationship. In John's conclusions—he has two—he said that there are many other things he could have written or said about Jesus. But he chose these stories because they tell who Jesus was and is.

For myself, I turn to the stories of rescue. I tell about the time we were down to $75 and then the job came. I tell stories of healing, of the time we prayed for our son's leg to grow and it miraculously did. I relive the stories of grace, the sins that should have shamed and destroyed me but mercifully didn't. And I tell of the times when I sat to listen, and he spoke, just like a friend.

1. **What stories do you tell about Jesus when you talk to others? To what events do you turn, to remind yourself of Jesus's power and authority?**

John is careful to explain that there was one who turned him toward Jesus. John the Baptist was the prophet who gave the apostle John the ability to see the true Messiah. I, too, had prophets who shared Jesus with me until I could see for myself.

My parents and grandparents introduced me to the Savior. My best friend in high school helped me stand firm in the faith of Jesus. The cute college guy across from me at Wendy's demonstrated the importance of the written Word to understand the Living Word.

2. **Who are your prophets? Who brought you the message that Jesus is the Christ, the Son of God? To whom are you being a prophet?**

The apostle John tells us many times that people didn't know who Jesus was. The crowds asked for a sign, even after they were fed in a stunningly miraculous way. The Pharisees asked for proof of his identity, but he offered none that they could comprehend. Even Philip, Jesus's own disciple, asked him for a foolproof sign.

And John the Baptist, Jesus's cousin, admitted that he wasn't sure Jesus was who he said he was until the sign of the baptism.

It was through Jesus's baptism that John said the Chosen One had been revealed. Baptism revealed Jesus's true identity.

My own baptism was not a sudden realization of who I was and am. It was the beginning of a process of accepting my new identity. It was the first of many stepping-stones on the pathway to God.

But like John and Andrew, baptism is what made me aware of the need for something more. John the Baptist wasn't enough for these two. They wanted the real thing.

3. **What was your first step toward Jesus? What convinced you that where you were wasn't where you wanted to be?**

✤ ACTION ✤

1. Share the beginning of your story with someone. How did you discover Jesus? What was the first sign for you? What stories continue to convince you that you made the right decision?

2. Invite friends to a campfire. Tell the stories that you want others to remember. My own stories include rescue from situations, disease, and sinfulness. What is your story? If you can't participate in a campfire, try a roomful of candles.

3. Ask another believer about their story. Encourage them to share their background with you. Ask how and where they found Jesus. Find out what made them believe in the Messiah.

CHAPTER 2

HE PARTIES

✛ A REUNION ✛

"Tell us about the disciples," urged a young man sitting halfway back.

John glanced at him and smiled. "We were brothers, all of us," he began.

"Like me and Paul." Caleb smiled up at his mother.

"Shh," she hushed him, though she nodded in agreement.

"Some of us were born brothers," John went on, "and others were made brothers. Andrew thought that the baptizing prophet John was the Messiah, but John kept denying it. When John saw Jesus walking by and proclaimed him the Lamb of God, there wasn't any holding Andrew back. I remember it was about the tenth hour and Jesus let us join him for the rest of the day. He gave us bread and fish for supper, and then said he would make us fishers of men if we would join him. Andrew ran like a lamb out to pasture to tell his brother, Simon, that we'd found the Messiah.

"My brother, James, was skinning some fish for our mother when I told him we'd found the real thing. Simon and my brother joined us that night, and we all sat up into the early hours of the morning talking and listening to Jesus. The next day was foggy, and we couldn't get out to fish, so Peter and Andrew came over to our house and we discussed what we should do. Finally the four of us went back to Jesus and asked if we could stay with him like Andrew had stayed with John. Jesus agreed, but he didn't spread honey on any of it. He said it wouldn't be any easier a life than one with John had been. He planned to be on the move a lot, and we would miss our families as well as many meals."

Caleb's mom brushed his hair with her lips, and hugged him tight on her lap.

"Perhaps to prove his point, Jesus said that he wanted to go first to Galilee and that he was leaving in the morning. He had some family friends getting married, and he was going to the wedding. We were invited to follow along, including Philip. We were all from Bethsaida and knew each other growing up. It was fun at first, traveling along and enjoying each other's company. And the wedding turned out to be more interesting than we had expected, as—"

"Whoa! This is my story," declared a woman with graying hair. Her eyes reflected the fire's bright light. She jumped up from the middle of the throng of children, revealing a small frame, barely larger than a child's and just as agile.

"Yes, it is, Junia," John agreed as he welcomed the woman and then put an arm protectively around her shoulders. "Would you mind sharing it with our friends?" He smiled, gesturing toward the crowd.

"I would be delighted," she answered. "I was as nervous as a chicken on butchering day," Junia began. "I remember the butterflies swirling around my insides, and my hands and feet sweating like crazy. I had met my husband twice before, but we hardly knew each other. Abram was from Cana, and I was from Nazareth. He was quite a bit older, though still handsome and ruddy. He was a shepherd and goatherd, but he never smelled bad." The woman giggled like a young girl.

A salty breeze blew in from the water and she breathed deeply. Her smile was infectious; all the women laughed knowingly. Caleb looked around in confusion and then laughed along.

"My mother dressed me that day. I had a red robe with tiny green leaves embroidered around the sleeves and hem. Mother had spent many hours on it at night to be a surprise for me. Mary, Jesus's mother, was our neighbor. She helped me get ready too. She brushed my hair and then braided it in coils around my head. Mother gave me her own gold pins, and Mary used them to fasten the braids under my veil.

"Then we took the cart to ride to Cana. Papa seemed very stern and I thought he was angry with me, but later I saw him crying when the wedding was over." Junia's voice softened. "We arrived before lunch, and Abram's mother ushered all of us into the women's quarters before the men could see us. Abram's family wasn't rich, but they had plenty, and the table was filled with dainty pies and pastries. His mother was an excellent cook, and she had taught her servants well." Junia nodded.

"There was music and food all afternoon. The rabbi was a large man, and he laughed all the time. He helped me relax as he spoke with Mother and the other women about the ceremony. Then the music started, and it was all a blur. There was dancing, and singing, and lots and lots of eating and drinking. People seemed to be coming out of the woodwork; I was overwhelmed trying to remember everyone's name."

She threw her arms up in the air and laughed like a child. Her teeth were straight and white, glistening in the firelight. She hugged herself and took a deep breath. She exhaled and looked at everyone.

"Papa sat at the head table with Abram, greeting everyone. Papa was happy to see how respected Abram's family was by the people in the village. There were people from Nazareth and Cana, of course, but many others came from the villages all around.

"Several days into the celebration I was tired from all the excitement, so I excused myself for a rest in the ladies' quarters. On my way out I heard a commotion in the kitchen. Amilia, one of the servants, was exclaiming over the large crowd of people and telling the cook that they were out of wine." Junia's eyes grew large as an owl's.

"Naturally I was embarrassed. Papa would be ashamed in front of all these people to discover he had given his daughter to a man who couldn't provide enough wine for the wedding. Mary found me crying and I told her what was going on. She said she would handle it, and then took off, looking for Jesus."

The older woman looked around at the listeners and raised her shoulders, implying the absurdity of looking for a guest in the middle of such a crisis.

"Mm, mm, mm." Several of the ladies acknowledged the seriousness of the situation and shook their heads.

"Mary told me later that Jesus was reluctant to help because he didn't want to steal the show, but you know how persuasive mothers can be." Junia laughed. "Jesus told Amilia and Havilah to fill the large ceremonial washing jars with water and then to take some of the water to my father. I wasn't too sure about that. I was certain Papa would spit it out, but instead he smiled and licked his lips. Abram even said Papa proclaimed it the best wine he had ever had!" Junia beamed.

The crowd cheered and stomped their feet.

Caleb looked around at everyone and started clapping his hands. "Why are we cheering, Mama?" he asked.

"Jesus performed a miracle. He turned water into wine."

Caleb's mouth dropped open, and he continued applauding. Junia bowed slightly and weaved her way back into the children's sitting area. When she sat down, only her gray hair gave away her age.

Two women carrying large water jars walked into the circle. They offered a ladle of water first to John, who gulped it in long slurps, and then passed the ladles around to the other men.

A woman approached John and asked if she might share her story next. A wide stump was brought near the fire and placed on end for her to be seated. The drinking and stretching ended once everyone was served, and the boisterous conversations died down to a few scattered whispers.

"Who is she, Mama?" young Caleb asked, burrowing his face in his mother's shoulder. The break had helped to wake him, but time was marching into the deep darkness of night and his eyelids felt heavy.

"That is Philomena, the next storyteller," his weary mother replied. "Listen."

"I didn't know Jesus, but my mother did," the woman began. "My mother was beautiful, a tall, willowy woman with long, silky hair and a smile like the noonday sun. It was believed that my mother was cursed because she only bore daughters and her husbands died one after another without heirs, but I remember the good years when she laughed and sang. Her first husband fell ill and died one month after she was married. My father, Philemon, was her second husband. Papa was a fisherman and a good provider. He treated us well and he loved my mother. Papa drowned in a storm, and I was married very early because Mother couldn't care for me. I regretted leaving my mother there. I knew she was unhappy." Philomena looked away from the listening crowd. "Mama took in sewing and tried to manage, but the rumors had begun. Sometimes I would hear news about Mama; it worried me. But I felt relieved that I was safe. I served my mother-in-law until I was old enough to be a wife to Thomas.

"My husband's family offered for Mother to stay with us, but she was still a beautiful woman, and a man in Sychar, who didn't care about the silly superstitions, quickly married her. Mother bore him two daughters and a son. The son was stillborn. Mother nearly died of heartache. Death had visited her too many times. I stayed with her for a while to help her heal and to care for my sisters. Her husband was kind and hopeful that there would be more sons, but it was not to be. He died from illness a year later."

The wind whispered in the trees as clouds played hide-and-seek with the moon and stars. The moaning of a sagging branch made Caleb shiver.

"My sisters were not old enough to marry. I was expecting my first child, so they came to stay with me and help. Mother married a tavern owner in Sychar, and they seemed well-suited for each other. He was old but kind, and he was gentle with Mother. He was gentle in all his ways, and that seemed to be his undoing. One night some bandits robbed the tavern and killed him. They attacked Mother and ruined her. They cut her face and arms. It was terrible." Philomena shuddered and wrapped her arms around herself.

An old woman sitting on the end of the bench with Caleb and his mother went to Philomena and rubbed her back and shoulders.

Philomena smiled softly at her and then cleared her throat. "My mother died that night. Not physically, but her spirit was gone. There was too much pain to bear. A farmer took pity on her and married her so that she wouldn't starve, but there wasn't any love between them. Finally the farmer couldn't stand her sadness any longer and sent her away. He kept my sisters as his wives, though, to show he had no ill will toward my mother." Philomena spit on the ground.

"She lived with a man in town who needed a housekeeper, but he refused to marry her. I suppose I understand." Philomena sighed. "But it disappointed me. The people of Sychar avoided Mother. They thought she was cursed, or else an evil witch. Either way they feared her, and she had no friends.

"I visited Mother whenever I could," Philomena assured the crowd as she shifted her weight on the stump. "Once, after planting, I went to see her. She was different, almost herself again. She told me that she had met a man named Jesus and that he had told her all she had ever done. She had gone to the village well to fill the large water jars when she met this strange man who spoke to her. He knew about all her husbands, even the one who wasn't a husband, and he hadn't run away in fright. In fact he had invited her to bring the man to him to talk with him." She smiled.

"Mother left her jar there to go back to town. She told everyone she had found the Messiah." Philomena grinned. "Jesus's disciples had already been in town buying food at the tavern, so the people knew something was up. The whole town came out to see this man, and they ended up inviting him to stay. Mother was so proud that Jesus stayed at her house without ever being afraid or disgusted. He stayed for two whole days." Philomena nodded for emphasis.

"Everyone in town listened to Jesus and what he had to say. All who heard him were intrigued and believed he was the Messiah. Mother said he filled her water jars with life as sweet as wine. She died just a few years later, but the time she had left was filled with joy as deep as a river."

"Your mother was a lovely woman," John said to Philomena. "I remember her talking with Jesus when we returned from town. I was excited to show Jesus the cucumbers we were given when we bought bread. I couldn't believe someone would just give them to us. The people of Sychar were very generous," he added, looking out at the gathering.

"Anyway," John continued, "I urged Jesus to try the cucumbers. I knew he was weary and had to be hungry, but he said he had food that we didn't know about. I was sure he hadn't been hiding food from us, so I thought maybe Philomena's mother had brought him food at the well. Soon all the people of Sychar joined us. Jesus picked up one of my cucumbers and inspected it. Then, looking at the gathering crowd, he said, 'Open your eyes and look at the fields. They are ripe for harvest!' Two days later I understood what he meant."

Caleb yawned as Philomena stood. The story had been too long for him and his head had nodded to his chest several times.

Philomena rubbed her lower back, and John suggested they call it a night.

Caleb's father gathered him off his mother's lap and headed toward the house they would be sharing with friends. His mother took Paul by the hand and fell in line shuffling to the door.

✤ An Ancient Story ✤
(John 2 and 4:1-42)

Actions speak louder than words. One person complains about the garbage along the side of the road; another spends Saturday picking up trash. A politician tweets sound bites about the expense of medication while a doctor goes the extra mile to fill out paperwork and get free prescriptions for patients. A preacher pounds the podium condemning sexual sin in a fiery sermon, and a college grad student spends Friday nights passing out bag lunches to prostitutes and offering a listening ear.

In the story of the wedding at Cana, which you're about to read, Jesus used religious vessels to make something good even better. Teaching and preaching are good ways to educate the population, but it is through action that people experience change. Judaism had become a set of rules and rituals instead of life- and soul-changing behaviors.

Notice how Jesus extended the scope of religious vessels in these stories: The water containers were for religious washing. And the well in Sychar belonged to one of the patriarchs of the Jewish religion.

1. **How did John use water in these stories to focus on Jesus's purpose or goal?**

John's second chapter opens at the wedding on what is the seventh day in his gospel. Everything had been set in order, and now it was time for Jesus to declare who he was. His first miracle was to turn water to wine, but not just any water. The water was taken from the ceremonial washing jars. Jesus was ready to cleanse his people, from the inside out.

The Jews watched for the Messiah for many years. As the Roman Empire stretched its reach and its requirements, the Jews watched even harder. They knew the Messiah would come with the richness of wine. Isaiah 25:6 says there will be a banquet of wine. Jeremiah 31:12 talks about the great joy that will accompany the Messiah, including new wine. Amos 9:13-14 says that new wine will drip from the mountains and flow through the hills.

2. **What did this miracle mean to those who knew where the wine came from? In what ways does your life flow with the new wine of Jesus?**

John didn't talk about miracles in his gospel. He showed us signs. To John a sign was more than a miracle. A miracle lasts for a little while, but the healed will fall sick again, the fed will get hungry again. A sign points to something.

In Exodus 7, God told Moses to go tell Pharaoh whom he was dealing with, and the way to tell him was with a sign. Moses was commanded to turn the Nile water—and all the water in buckets and stone jars—to blood. By this sign would Pharaoh know who God is.

John also believed that signs tell us who Jesus is. After this first sign—turning water to wine—the disciples believed in Jesus. What exactly they believed is uncertain. They didn't understand everything, because at the cross they all deserted him. But every belief must have a starting point, and the disciples' was in the water and wine.

3. What was your starting point?

Scarlett O'Hara would have understood the woman at the well. Scarlett was an Irish woman in the Deep South where Irish were unwelcome. She was a businesswoman at a time when working women were considered uncouth. She ran the business with ruthless ambition and loved another woman's husband. She was hated, despised, and considered sinful.

A basic summary of the Samaritans is that they were the resettled peoples of foreign conquests. They married into the local people groups, knowing God and gods. In Ezra 9, we get a sense of the great shame and distaste the Israelites had about the people of Samaria. It says they "mingled the holy race with the peoples around them" (v. 2 NIV).

Alexander the Great built a temple for the Samaritans on Mount Gerazim. John Hyrcanus, who was the ruler of Judea and also high priest from 134-104 BC, successfully enlarged the territory of Judea. He conquered Samaria and Idumea and forced the Idumeans to become Jewish. He destroyed the Samaritan temple on Mount Gerazim in 128 BC.

So when Jesus, a Jewish man, stopped and asked for a drink from a Samaritan woman of disrepute, you could have cut the tension with a knife. As you read, try to feel her animosity. And notice the disciples' response. Can you feel their eyes shifting from one to the other? The rules were about to be broken, and the result was an entire village's belief.

JOHN 2

¹ On the third day there was a wedding at Cana in Galilee, and the mother of Jesus was there. ² Jesus also was invited to the wedding with his disciples. ³ When the wine ran out, the mother of Jesus said to him, "They have no wine." ⁴ And Jesus said to her, "Woman, what does this have to do with me? My hour has not yet come." ⁵ His mother said to the servants, "Do whatever he tells you."

⁶ Now there were six stone water jars there for the Jewish rites of purification, each holding twenty or thirty gallons. ⁷ Jesus said to the servants, "Fill the jars with water." And they filled them up to the brim. ⁸ And he said to them, "Now draw some out and take it to the master of the feast." So they took it. ⁹ When the master of the feast tasted the water now become wine, and did not know where it came from (though the servants who had drawn the water knew), the master of the feast called the bridegroom ¹⁰ and said to him, "Everyone serves the good wine first, and when people have drunk freely, then the poor wine. But you have kept the good wine until now." ¹¹ This, the first of his signs, Jesus did at Cana in Galilee, and manifested his glory. And his disciples believed in him.

¹² After this he went down to Capernaum, with his mother and his brothers and his disciples, and they stayed there for a few days.

¹³ The Passover of the Jews was at hand, and Jesus went up to Jerusalem. ¹⁴ In the temple he found those who were selling oxen and sheep and pigeons, and the money-changers sitting there. ¹⁵ And making a whip of

cords, he drove them all out of the temple, with the sheep and oxen. And he poured out the coins of the money-changers and overturned their tables. ¹⁶ And he told those who sold the pigeons, "Take these things away; do not make my Father's house a house of trade." ¹⁷ His disciples remembered that it was written, "Zeal for your house will consume me."

¹⁸ So the Jews said to him, "What sign do you show us for doing these things?" ¹⁹ Jesus answered them, "Destroy this temple, and in three days I will raise it up." ²⁰ The Jews then said, "It has taken forty-six years to build this temple, and will you raise it up in three days?" ²¹ But he was speaking about the temple of his body. ²² When therefore he was raised from the dead, his disciples remembered that he had said this, and they believed the Scripture and the word that Jesus had spoken.

²³ Now when he was in Jerusalem at the Passover Feast, many believed in his name when they saw the signs that he was doing. ²⁴ But Jesus on his part did not entrust himself to them, because he knew all people ²⁵ and needed no one to bear witness about man, for he himself knew what was in man.

JOHN 4:1-42

¹ Now when Jesus learned that the Pharisees had heard that Jesus was making and baptizing more disciples than John ² (although Jesus himself did not baptize, but only his disciples), ³ he left Judea and departed again for

Galilee. ⁴ And he had to pass through Samaria. ⁵ So he came to a town of Samaria called Sychar, near the field that Jacob had given to his son Joseph. ⁶ Jacob's well was there; so Jesus, wearied as he was from his journey, was sitting beside the well. It was about the sixth hour.

⁷ A woman from Samaria came to draw water. Jesus said to her, "Give me a drink." ⁸ (For his disciples had gone away into the city to buy food.) ⁹ The Samaritan woman said to him, "How is it that you, a Jew, ask for a drink from me, a woman of Samaria?" (For Jews have no dealings with Samaritans.) ¹⁰ Jesus answered her, "If you knew the gift of God, and who it is that is saying to you, 'Give me a drink,' you would have asked him, and he would have given you living water." ¹¹ The woman said to him, "Sir, you have nothing to draw water with, and the well is deep. Where do you get that living water? ¹² Are you greater than our father Jacob? He gave us the well and drank from it himself, as did his sons and his livestock." ¹³ Jesus said to her, "Everyone who drinks of this water will be thirsty again, ¹⁴ but whoever drinks of the water that I will give him will never be thirsty again. The water that I will give him will become in him a spring of water welling up to eternal life." ¹⁵ The woman said to him, "Sir, give me this water, so that I will not be thirsty or have to come here to draw water."

¹⁶ Jesus said to her, "Go, call your husband, and come here." ¹⁷ The woman answered him, "I have no husband." Jesus said to her, "You are right in saying, 'I have no husband'; ¹⁸ for you have had five husbands, and the one you now have is not your husband. What you have said is

true." [19] The woman said to him, "Sir, I perceive that you are a prophet. [20] Our fathers worshiped on this mountain, but you say that in Jerusalem is the place where people ought to worship." [21] Jesus said to her, "Woman, believe me, the hour is coming when neither on this mountain nor in Jerusalem will you worship the Father. [22] You worship what you do not know; we worship what we know, for salvation is from the Jews. [23] But the hour is coming, and is now here, when the true worshipers will worship the Father in spirit and truth, for the Father is seeking such people to worship him. [24] God is spirit, and those who worship him must worship in spirit and truth." [25] The woman said to him, "I know that Messiah is coming (he who is called Christ). When he comes, he will tell us all things." [26] Jesus said to her, "I who speak to you am he."

[27] Just then his disciples came back. They marveled that he was talking with a woman, but no one said, "What do you seek?" or, "Why are you talking with her?" [28] So the woman left her water jar and went away into town and said to the people, [29] "Come, see a man who told me all that I ever did. Can this be the Christ?" [30] They went out of the town and were coming to him.

[31] Meanwhile the disciples were urging him, saying, "Rabbi, eat." [32] But he said to them, "I have food to eat that you do not know about." [33] So the disciples said to one another, "Has anyone brought him something to eat?" [34] Jesus said to them, "My food is to do the will of him who sent me and to accomplish his work. [35] Do you not say, 'There are yet four months, then comes the harvest'? Look, I tell you, lift up your eyes, and see that the fields

are white for harvest. [36] Already the one who reaps is receiving wages and gathering fruit for eternal life, so that sower and reaper may rejoice together. [37] For here the saying holds true, 'One sows and another reaps.' [38] I sent you to reap that for which you did not labor. Others have labored, and you have entered into their labor."

[39] Many Samaritans from that town believed in him because of the woman's testimony, "He told me all that I ever did." [40] So when the Samaritans came to him, they asked him to stay with them, and he stayed there two days. [41] And many more believed because of his word. [42] They said to the woman, "It is no longer because of what you said that we believe, for we have heard for ourselves, and we know that this is indeed the Savior of the world."

✣ A MODERN STORY ✣

"I just want some peace."

Lights glared, cameras flashed, microphones waggled in front of the tall, young man. The police led him away. He was sentenced to fifteen life sentences in a Wisconsin prison.

Curt, a Christian in Oklahoma who had served four years in a Kansas prison for theft, watched that television interview. He understood the pain in the convict's eyes. *I know where you can get that peace in full, overflowing buckets.* He sent a Bible correspondence course to the Wisconsin prisoner.

Mary, a woman in Virginia, also saw the young man on television. *Such sorrow.* She, too, sent him Bible lessons.

To their surprise Curt and Mary received answers from the prisoner, Jeff. He had completed the course and lessons. He sent back the papers with a personal note. He had read and studied the materials and believed in the power of Jesus to forgive. Like the Ethiopian eunuch, he desired to be baptized, but the prison had no baptistery.

Curt and Mary began contacting ministers in Wisconsin. Would anyone be willing to help Jeff be baptized?

A few weeks later Roy, a minister in Wisconsin, found himself sitting at a table in the center of a prison's sterile visiting room. Roy's heart was pounding, and his hands were sweating. He'd never met with a prisoner before, never been inside a prison.

His anxiety was understandable. From 1978 to 1991, the man he was about to meet had killed and dismembered sixteen men. He had committed sexual acts with some of the corpses. Hidden their bones and body parts around his apartment. Eaten parts of the victims. This was not the type of person Roy encountered while spreading the Word of God in Wisconsin.

The door opened, and a tall, blond man entered. The guard pulled the door closed and left the two men alone.

"Thank you for meeting me," Jeff said. He looked down, his own fear and anxiety expressed in the stoop of his shoulders.

The two men talked for over an hour. Jeff had a knowledge of God, but had previously accepted the teaching of evolution and the denial of a higher being. Now he wasn't so sure.

"Evolution cheapens life," Jeff said. "If there's no higher purpose, no accountability, then you can do what you want to any other life. It doesn't matter."

Jeff had decided there is more beyond this life, and that he wanted to be a part of hope. He was afraid, though, that Roy wouldn't want to baptize him, that he would be considered too evil.

Roy studied the Bible with Jeff for several weeks. He felt that Jeff was sincere in his desire to accept Jesus's forgiveness. Roy contacted the prison chaplain, and they arranged to perform the baptism in the prison's medical unit hot tub. Jeff's lanky body curled into the fetal position as he was lowered under the water.

Jeff had committed heinous acts to gain power. "I never enjoyed the killing. It was a means to an end. I wanted the person under my complete control. I'm glad that it's over." His rebirth was as beautiful as the May flowers blooming outside.

Months passed, and Roy met weekly with Jeff. They continued to study the Bible, and Jeff began to teach others in prison about Jesus. He even spent his own money to buy Bible lessons for the other inmates. Jeff was excited to attend worship services in the prison on Sundays, the dark green prison uniforms unable to darken the light that had dawned in his own life.

It was only to last a few months. In July 1994, a fellow inmate attacked the infamous Jeffrey Dahmer with a metal bar and bludgeoned him to death.

Jeff had total peace at last.[1]

---

1   This section is based on material from the following sources:
Bobby Ross Jr., "Did 'Jailhouse Religion' Save Jeffrey Dahmer?," The Christian Chronicle, Aug. 1, 2010, accessed April 2017, christian-chronicle.org/did-jailhouse-religion-save-jeffrey-dahmer/.
"Confessions of a Serial Killer: Jeffrey Dahmer," Dateline, National Broadcasting Corporation, Feb. 1994, accessed April 2017, via Top Documentary Films, topdocumentaryfilms.com/confessions-of-a-serial-killer/.
Craig Spychalla, "Encounter with Dahmer Changed Minister's Life," The Christian Chronicle, Dec. 15, 2004, accessed April 2017, christian-chronicle.org/encounter-with-dahmer-changed-ministers-life/.

✢ REFLECTION ✢

My own wedding story involves a record-breaking blizzard, closed roads, frozen doors that wouldn't open, and walking through the snow and wind to get to the church on time. I can also tell you other couples' stories of wedding photographers that forgot the film, a bride that fainted and ended up in the emergency room, and a beach wedding that sandblasted the guests. Weddings are best imperfect; the happy couple will have a story to tell for the rest of their lives.

The wedding feast at Cana is a great example. People are still talking about it thousands of years later.

We don't know the bride and groom. We aren't sure why Jesus and his mother were there or why she was privy to the lack-of-wine incident. What we do know is that Jesus was filling the most basic need in life with his sweetness.

Many people turn this story into teachings about alcohol consumption or Mary's authority or even the church's role in a marriage. Don't dwell on those things but notice instead what happened as a result.

Belief in Jesus.

―――

"Your friend, Jean, called." Matt looked at me and I knew what was coming next. "She doesn't look like her voice, does she?"

I laughed out loud.

Jean is about five-ten with broad shoulders and solid feet. Matt had only seen pictures, never heard the high-pitched, childlike voice. When she called and left a message, well, it was unexpected.

There are rules in life. Very seldom do we like surprises. Spring follows winter, dogs chase cats, fish live in the sea, and religion is structured—rules that cannot be broken.

But we all experience an occasional warm winter day. Some dogs sit on the porch while a cat snuggles on the rocker. There are ponds, oceans, and rivers teeming with fish. And religion sometimes gets scrubbed and polished to reveal the truth under a coat of grime.

At the wedding in Cana, Jesus told the servants to fill six stone water jars that were used for ceremonial washing. Jews would use these jars for the elaborate washing rituals required by the Pharisees. Later, when Jesus drank the wine at Passover, he declared the Passover wine his blood that washes away the sins of man. Water to wine to blood.

John says the changing of the water to wine in the stone jars was Jesus's first sign. It was what convinced the disciples that they better pay attention. It was the beginning of the end—the end of religion as they knew it.

But if that was unexpected, what followed in Sychar was even more so. Not only was this new way offered to the outsider Samaritans, it was offered to one whom they believed God had cursed.

No one knows for sure about the men connected to the woman at the well. Some conjecture that they represent the six gods of the area—gods the Samaritans turned to instead of Yahweh. Some say she was a prostitute, a divorcee perhaps. Maybe she was like Hosea's wife, Gomer, who cheated on her husband. And why did she not marry the sixth man? Would he not have her, or was it her decision not to marry?

Try to ignore those questions and look at Jesus's actions. He talked to her, even asked her help. He offered her something she wanted. And he offered to share it with the man as well. He did the unexpected.

1. **How is Jesus different from what your religion or church teaches you?**
2. **In what ways is Jesus better than the religious rituals you have been offered before?**
3. **What unexpected thing has Jesus done for you?**

In the book of John, between the story of the wedding at Cana and the woman at the well in Sychar, there is a story about a man named Nicodemus. He was a religious man, and he had been watching Jesus. He had seen, or at least heard of, the miracles that Jesus was performing. He came at night, fearful and yet longing, to discuss Jesus's teaching.

Jesus told him some strange things:

Jesus replied, "Very truly I tell you, no one can see the kingdom of God unless they are born again."

"How can someone be born when they are old?" Nicodemus asked. "Surely they cannot enter a second time into their mother's womb to be born!"

Jesus answered, "Very truly I tell you, no one can enter the kingdom of God unless they are born of water and the Spirit. Flesh gives birth to flesh, but the Spirit gives birth to spirit. You should not be surprised at my saying, 'You must be born again.' The wind blows wherever it pleases. You hear its sound, but you cannot tell where it comes from or where it is going. So it is with everyone born of the Spirit."

"How can this be?" Nicodemus asked.

"You are Israel's teacher," said Jesus, "and do you not understand these things? Very truly I tell you, we speak of what we know, and we testify to what we have seen, but still you people do not accept our testimony. I have spoken to you of earthly things and you do not believe; how then will you believe if I speak of heavenly things? No one has ever gone into heaven except the one who came from heaven—the Son of Man. Just as Moses lifted up the snake in the wilderness, so the Son of Man must be lifted up, that everyone who believes may have eternal life in him."

For God so loved the world that he gave his one and only Son, that whoever believes in him shall not perish but have eternal life. For God did not send his Son into the world to condemn the world, but to save the world through him. Whoever believes in him is not condemned, but whoever does not believe stands condemned already because they have not believed in the name of God's one and only Son. This is the verdict: Light has come into the world, but people loved darkness instead of light because their deeds were evil. Everyone who does evil hates the light, and will not come into the light for fear that their deeds will be exposed. But whoever lives by the truth comes into the light, so that it may be seen plainly that what they have done has been done in the sight of God. (John 3:3-21 NIV)

Nicodemus came in darkness. The woman at the well came in the middle of the day. One turned away from Jesus; the other brought an entire village. Remember the prologue in John's first chapter? "The light shines in the darkness."

Jesus told Nicodemus that he came to bring light and truth into the world. This light was offered to Nicodemus, a religious teacher, but it is also offered to any who are willing to come into the light.

Sometimes we look at people and judge whether they will want to hear about Jesus before we ever tell them anything. Most wouldn't have expected that the Samaritan woman would be the one to take Jesus at his word. And most wouldn't have thought that a serial killer would want anything to do with the light of Christ.

4. **Do you ever turn away from sharing the life of Jesus with someone because you think that they wouldn't want to hear?**

5. **Is it possible that you have judged someone to be "too evil" for the saving grace of Jesus? Do you truly believe that Jesus came for "whoever"?**

There is something that these stories have in common. The disciples believed in Jesus when they saw the water turned to wine, and they followed, sharing the message with others. The woman at the well believed Jesus and shared the good news with her town. Jeffrey Dahmer believed Jesus and began telling other inmates about the grace of God. It seems that believing Jesus is like having a zucchini garden in July: you share with everyone.

6. **Have you been so overwhelmed with the goodness of Jesus that you share with others? Have you told the teller at the bank how much Jesus loves her? What about the green-haired, tattooed teen next door?**

✠ ACTION ✠

1. Enter a side of town where you don't feel comfortable. Walk through it, as Jesus and his disciples walked through Samaria, and look for the fields ready for harvest. Remember that Jesus said the fields were ready before he ever taught the people of Sychar. Ask God to show you which people are thirsty. But don't be surprised if it's someone who looks like "the wrong sort."

2. Offer to help someone outside of your circle of friends. Share the love of Jesus with the single mom who needs a break by taking the kids for dinner and giving her a night off. Mow your Muslim neighbor's yard in the name of Jesus. Serve at the soup kitchen and sit down with the clients. Whoever it is, don't let their looks or their behavior convince you they don't want Jesus. They might be dying of thirst right at the well.

3. Do you know someone in jail? Visit them, write to them, talk to them about Jesus. Do you know a leader at your church? Talk to them about Jesus too. It will refill their own well.

CHAPTER 3

HE HEALS

✣ A REUNION ✣

The morning mist was beginning to burn off. Caleb could see another fishing boat sailing beside the one he was in. A third boat trailed just behind, carrying the women. This was the first time Caleb was allowed to sail with the men on a fishing expedition. Papa said it was just a short trip, to get breakfast for everyone.

A man's voice drifted through the haze that slithered around the boats. Caleb spotted the man sitting near John.

"I was a servant in the house of Fabius, one of Herod's officials, but my story really starts at Peter's house. Peter's mother-in-law, Sarah, was a friend of my mother's. They grew up together and our families remained friends. Sarah's daughter married Peter when we were young. I had hoped …" He stared at the ship floor. "But my father had little to offer me, and I was sent to be a servant in Fabius's house. I didn't mind, not really. Herod Antipas was a kind king, and Fabius was a good master.

"Sarah became ill soon after Peter started following Jesus, and word got out pretty quick that Jesus had healed her. So naturally when my master's son fell ill, and no medicines helped, I urged him to contact Jesus." He glanced at John for approval.

"It was the right thing to do, Nahshon," John said, pulling his cloak tighter.

Nahshon went on, "Fabius sent me to Peter's house to find out where Jesus was. I knew Peter had gone to Jerusalem earlier, so it was with trepidation that I asked Sarah where Jesus could be found. I was elated when she told me they had gone to Cana. My master was waiting at the gate when I returned. The fever was growing worse; the boy was gasping for breath. Fabius was so relieved to hear that Jesus was close by that he mounted the horse himself and rode furiously to Cana, desperate to bring back Jesus.

"When he got to Cana, no one seemed to know where Jesus was. My master searched all over until someone told him to look at Nathanael's house. Jesus was there speaking to a crowd in the shade of an orchard. The crowd parted to let Fabius pass. Later I heard that people thought he was possessed, his eyes were so wild. But you see, the boy was his only son and he loved him so much. He was a desperate man." Nahshon's hands shook as he recalled the events. He pointed toward Caleb. "He was just a little man, like you.

"Fabius begged Jesus to return with him to Capernaum. He even offered to buy a horse right then for him, so they could ride faster, but Jesus ignored his pleas. 'I'm not a show pony,' Jesus told him. 'My signs and wonders are not a magic act to make you believe.'

"'I'm not here for a show,' Fabius defended himself. 'I just want my son back!' So many tears flooded his cheeks, they muddied the ground where he stood. Jesus took him into the house and gave him some water. 'Go home,' he told my master. 'Your son will live.'

"Meanwhile we were all back at the house hoping for some improvement in the boy. He hadn't eaten in days and not even water would stay in him. But just about the time we gave up all hope, his appearance changed. His chest stopped heaving and the tension in his muscles relaxed. His mother, Anna, smoothed his hair and washed his face. The fever was gone. Anna sent me to tell Fabius to come back home, that all was well.

"Ephraim, another servant, and I ran like gazelles to tell our master the good news. We were so happy that we ran for an hour before we slowed. Fabius came riding upon us and we called out, 'He lives! Master, your son is well!'" Nahshon's face glowed.

Caleb clapped his hands and bounced on the bench.

"Fabius asked us when the fever had left, and we told him only an hour before, at one o'clock. Then Fabius fell from his horse and prostrated himself on the ground. 'I have seen the Holy One,' he cried. Then he mounted and rode off to the house. By the time we returned, everyone knew the story. All of us believed ... and do to this day," he finished, slapping his chest.

✠ An Ancient Story ✠
(John 4:43-54)

In the reading section that follows, notice that Jesus was sought by a "royal official." He was probably one of Herod Antipas's officials, though Herod was officially a tetrarch and not a king.

This was the same Herod who had ordered the beheading of John the Baptist. In Luke 13, Jesus was told that Herod wanted to kill him, and then in Luke 23, Jesus stood in front of Herod before his death. How much Herod knew of Jesus at the time of this passage in John's gospel is uncertain. However, it is certain that Jesus knew how their relationship would develop, and he didn't let it stop him from helping Herod's official.

Jesus had just spent several days with the Samaritans, a group snubbed by the Jews, as they questioned and learned from his teachings. He left the warm fuzzies of foreign Samaria for the cold greeting of his own region, Galilee. Then another outsider approached him. Just as the Samaritan woman believed right away, this royal official took Jesus at his word and believed in Jesus's power.

Sometimes Christians imagine that "foreign" people—those with different values, beliefs, or customs—don't want what Jesus has to offer, yet it was the outsiders whom John portrayed as seekers.

1. **Who are the foreigners in your life?**

In verse 48, Jesus talked to the official, but he was speaking to the crowd. In America we might say *y'all, you'uns, yous,* or even *you all.* The NIV translates it "you people." Whichever way you want to read it, Jesus was addressing the crowd and telling them he wasn't there to be their magician or show pony. He accused them of wanting to see signs and wonders. This is the only place in John's gospel that this word is used for *wonders,* as if the people had come for a carnival act.

But the royal official was not daunted. He begged for Jesus to heal his son. Jesus understands deep pain, and he obliged.

He didn't argue. He didn't demand payment or withhold his power. He didn't chastise or sermonize. He healed.

2. **Have you ever come to Jesus this desperate? What was the result?**

In 2 Kings 5, Naaman, a foreign military leader, suffered from leprosy. A servant girl captured from the Israelites told Naaman's wife that there was a prophet in Israel who could heal Naaman. Long story short, Naaman got permission and visited Elisha the prophet. Elisha told the man to go dip in the Jordan river, and Naaman pitched a fit because he wanted Elisha to do a song and dance to heal him, at least wave his arms. I'm not joking; go read it.

In ancient times it was common for healers to touch the afflicted. We often read of Jesus touching the sick. He put his fingers in the deaf man's ears. He spit and rubbed mud on the blind man's eyes. But for the royal official, he stayed put.

This guy had clout. He could have demanded Jesus accompany him. Instead he showed respect: "Sir, come down before my child dies."

Jesus accepted the man's pleas and healed the child on the spot. No touching, no spitting, not even a wave of the hand.

The man took Jesus at his word.

3. **Do you? If not, what are you having difficulty believing?**

JOHN 4:43-54

[43] After the two days he departed for Galilee. [44] (For Jesus himself had testified that a prophet has no honor

in his own hometown.) [45] So when he came to Galilee, the Galileans welcomed him, having seen all that he had done in Jerusalem at the feast. For they too had gone to the feast.

[46] So he came again to Cana in Galilee, where he had made the water wine. And at Capernaum there was an official whose son was ill. [47] When this man heard that Jesus had come from Judea to Galilee, he went to him and asked him to come down and heal his son, for he was at the point of death. [48] So Jesus said to him, "Unless you see signs and wonders you will not believe." [49] The official said to him, "Sir, come down before my child dies." [50] Jesus said to him, "Go; your son will live." The man believed the word that Jesus spoke to him and went on his way. [51] As he was going down, his servants met him and told him that his son was recovering. [52] So he asked them the hour when he began to get better, and they said to him, "Yesterday at the seventh hour the fever left him." [53] The father knew that was the hour when Jesus had said to him, "Your son will live." And he himself believed, and all his household. [54] This was now the second sign that Jesus did when he had come from Judea to Galilee.

✚ A MODERN STORY ✚

I met her at a meeting for Women of Westminster (WOW). Our husbands attended the same seminary. She was kind; I was confused. The topic was unfamiliar: mortification of the body. I came from a different Christian tradition, and though I could deduce that they were talking about the death of the body,

I wasn't sure why. It was to be the theme for the lecture series, and I remember asking, "Is this really a concern?"

The tall, slender brunette that sat near me tried to translate across denominational divides. Her name was Beth. We became friends, not just at WOW meetings, but also at park playdates.

Little did we know that mortification would soon become a painfully personal topic.

A year or so later I was expecting my second child. My friend, Beth, was also expecting her second a few days before me. My pregnancy was uneventful. Hers was terribly not so.

Beth never had an ultrasound with her first child, so when an ultrasound was scheduled for this pregnancy, she and her husband were excited. She was about sixteen weeks along in July of 1998. The nurse's expression was as cold as the gel on Beth's tiny, rounded belly. They were quickly rushed into the doctor's office.

Steven and Beth Badorf didn't understand the words the doctor was telling them. They knew it was serious. They knew there was danger. They were scheduled for further tests and sent home.

Their baby girl had an omphalocele. Her internal organs were developing outside of the abdominal cavity. Surgery was a possibility, but first there had to be tests, as omphaloceles often present with other birth defects.

Beth and Steven spent a weekend praying and fasting to see if they should permit the amniocentesis. They feared the risks of the test. After a weekend of mutual silence they rejoined on Monday and both felt God leading them to undergo the test.

The results came during a reunion in August. Trisomy 18 was one of the worst diagnoses possible. Most babies with trisomy 18, if they even make it to birth, live only a few days.

Sudden death occurs due to heart failure, respiratory failure, or a neurological issue. Those at the reunion prayed and cried with Beth and Steven, but the anguished couple didn't remember any of it. They were heartbroken.

Beth and Steven were referred to a research hospital and told to abort their baby. That wasn't an option for them. A friend suggested a doctor at St. Christopher's Hospital for Children. She was a believer. They would try.

They sat in the small office, the smell of antiseptic unable to remove the scent of fear. Their first child, a son, was strong and healthy. There was no family history of birth defects. Why was this happening?

When Beth saw the little lady walk in, dressed all in black and wearing sensible shoes, she couldn't believe this was a world-renowned neonatologist. As the doctor sat down to visit, Steven and Beth began to relax. The doctor suggested that all anyone wants in life is to love and to be loved. Surely they could do that much for this little girl that God was giving them.

The first problem to overcome was that St. Christopher's couldn't deliver the baby. Children's hospitals don't have maternity wards. Beth and Steven had to find a hospital willing to deliver what was considered a "nonviable life form." They were told by doctors that a C-section would not be performed because it would needlessly submit Beth to surgery, and the possibility of the omphalocele breaking would also put Beth in danger. Abortion was still considered their only legitimate option.

Finally a hospital in the area agreed to deliver, and a C-section was scheduled for December 18. Beth would deliver and recover at the hospital for forty-eight hours, while Steven would accompany Baby Abigail to St. Christopher's.

God's plans, though, are seldom the same as our own. Early on December 15, Beth went into labor. They rushed to the hospital, where several teams of doctors were supposed to be prepared for this very unusual delivery. Instead there was chaos.

By the time it was mostly straightened out, Beth was fully dilated and effaced. Abigail was born at six in the morning without a C-section and without a ruptured omphalocele. An hour later Steven and the baby were in an ambulance headed to St. Christopher's. Because she hadn't undergone a C-section, Beth was able to follow a few hours later. That afternoon she saw Abigail for the first time in the neonatal intensive care unit (NICU).

With Abigail under a warming lamp in the NICU, it became obvious that physically holding her improved her vital signs. The doctor in charge of the NICU was a visiting physician, but she was also a believer. She arranged for Abigail to be moved into a special step-down unit that was empty due to a hospital merger. The doctor suggested that people hold Abigail, and a call was sent out to church members and seminarians alike to come and hold this gift from God.

Beth and Steven told God, "We will hold her until we place her in your arms."

Over a hundred people came to hold the precious girl. The many empty hands also offered to hold other babies in the NICU who had no one visiting them. So many visited to help and pray and encourage that the staff thought it was a cult.

Abigail was born on a Tuesday. She opened her eyes on Thursday. But the doctor held no hope—"She will not go home." By Saturday she was showing signs of definite decline. Steven and Beth made the decision that afternoon to disconnect the breathing tube and IV.

The doctor assured them that instead of promoting life, the breathing tube and IV were only prolonging death. "I knew it was the right thing to do," says Beth, "but I still felt wrong about it. Was I killing my daughter?"

Abigail was held in her parents' arms until they placed her in the Father's arms at nine o'clock that evening. She lived less than five days.

Are you wondering how the story of a little girl's death is a sign that Jesus is the Messiah? It does seem out of place at first glance. Abigail's parents certainly struggled with it.

At church the congregation would chant, "God is good, all the time; all the time, God is good." Beth, however, cried out that God wasn't good. How could taking away her baby girl be good? It took fifteen long years before she could say "God is good" with conviction.

Beth believes that Abigail's short life was a gift to show her the sin and darkness that live in her own heart. Steven says, "Abigail was the greatest theologian I ever met; I sat under some of the best. ... But she never even opened her mouth."

A couple of years after Abigail's death, one of her doctors told Beth and Steven, "Her short life made more of an impact than mine ever will." Doctors and nurses still talk about when those crazy Jesus people came to love on a baby girl destined to die.

Over the years the Badorfs have been able to walk alongside other parents of children with trisomy 18. They have also counseled parents who have suddenly lost children. They have been able to offer grace and compassion to the hurting lives around them, and they have found forgiveness and love in their hearts for each other.

Just as the royal official in John took Jesus at his word and found his son alive and well, so Steven and Beth have found a word in Jesus as well. That word is "resurrection." The goodness of God doesn't always look the way we want it to look, but it always ends the way we want it to end:

Saved by the Messiah. Alive with the King.[1]

✣ REFLECTION ✣

John does not seem to be telling his story in chronological order. His main concern appears to be the signs that will remind or convince his readers of who Jesus was and is. Because of this it is likely that other healings also took place. The royal official had heard of Jesus and his miracles. Jesus chose Capernaum as his home place. Perhaps this official had met Jesus before, was even there when the paraplegic was lowered through the roof in a house in Capernaum.

If I were to share signs in my life of Jesus's power, I would talk about the times that God has spoken to me. I would include visions and actual voices. I would also include the answered prayers and the voices of others in my life. I would talk about gifts and blessings that appeared out of nowhere at just the right moment, like the time a woman stopped off at my house on a Sunday to deliver mail that had been incorrectly delivered to

---

1   This section is based on material from the following source:
Elizabeth and Steven Badorf, interview by Traci L. Stead, Aug. 1, 2017.

her the week before. The envelope was muddy and torn, so I have no doubt that it sat somewhere else for a long time as well. Inside the envelope was a check for fifty dollars. It just happened that I needed that fifty dollars the next day. No matter what order you tell your story, the important part is that it is told.

1. **What draws you to Jesus? What prompts you to turn to him in a time of crisis?**

In Matthew 13, Mark 6, and Luke 4, Jesus returned to his hometown of Nazareth. The people were surprised by his teaching abilities and stunned by his sayings. But their prejudice—"Isn't this the carpenter Joseph's son?"—wouldn't allow them to witness his true power. John alluded to this in chapter 4, verse 44.

2. **In what ways have you allowed your familiarity with the Son of God to overshadow your expectations of him? Is he able to perform miracles in your life?**

The royal official came from Capernaum to Cana to beg for his son's life. It is a day's walk uphill to Cana, about twenty to twenty-five miles. Certainly a royal official would have been able to send a servant to fetch Jesus. Instead the man went himself and pleaded for Jesus to come down to Capernaum with him.

In life there are prayers, and then there are begging, pleading, tearful prayers. There are times I offer heartfelt prayer, and there are times I fall on my face, cries of anguish strangling me as I beg for a blessing, for understanding. I can only imagine it was the latter that the royal official greeted Jesus with.

3. **When was the last time you put effort into your prayers?**

4. Have you gone out of your way to enter Jesus's presence?

5. Have you pleaded your cause, or have you just been a servant giving lip service?

In ancient times it was most common for a healer, or an article belonging to the healer, to touch the sick or afflicted. But according to chapter 20, John's gospel was written so that you may believe. What more definitive power is there than just speaking forth healing?

John tells us that the man took Jesus at his word and headed home. What great faith it must have taken to turn from the one he knew could help and start walking home. Beth and Steven, too, had great faith to fight for the child they expected would suffer and die. They took Jesus at his word that there are many mansions in heaven, and Abigail has a room waiting for them.

6. The holy scriptures are full of promises. Do you fully believe them? Enough to take Jesus at his word and confidently go on with your life?

✤ ACTION ✤

1. In a world of super-fast, super-powerful technology, it can be easy to trust in science and innovation. It is less easy to trust in the one who can heal without ever physically touching the injured, sick, diseased, or dying. Have you misplaced your trust? Spend some time examining your reactions to those who need God's healing touch. Have you been faithful in your prayers and your belief that God can heal, or have

you been faithless or forgetful of those who suffer? Consider adding a time of fasting and prayer to your week in honor of someone else's need.

2. Does your church have a list of sick and suffering members? Is your Facebook feed full of prayer requests from friends? Take a long walk, perhaps a walk uphill, until you are far away from home's comfort. Now fall at Jesus's feet and plead the cause of the sick. Beg for his mercy and his healing power in the lives of those you love.

3. Jesus scolded the royal official for seeking a sign and a wonder. The man assured Jesus that he was not looking for miracles just for the thrill of it. He wanted his son whole for the love of his son. Contemplate your own reasons for prayer requests you drop at the throne. Are you seeking signs and wonders, or are you painfully aware of brokenness and heartache? Are your requests selfishly motivated, or are they love-inhabited? Practice praying this week with an ear to your intentions.

CHAPTER 4

HE CONFRONTS

✛ A REUNION ✛

"I wish my story was so happy," James said. "It could have been, should have been. … But I always had a bad attitude about what happened."

The fog was burning off and the boats sat still on the placid waters. Limp nets hung over the sides waiting for the fish.

"Malchus and Simon were my best friends. We did everything together, including practical jokes." James winked at the boys. "We liked picking on a girl in town. She was beautiful, and every boy hoped for her. 'Stay behind the bushes until the chariot rounds the curve,' Malchus told me. He was a year older, so he got to be the boss."

Paul looked at Caleb and puffed out his chest. "See?"

"That's not fair," Caleb cried.

"Boys." Their mother's voice came across the water, her meaning loud and clear.

James held a gnarled finger to his lips and went on with his story. "I was laughing to myself thinking how Rhoda would scream when I jumped out at her. Then Malchus and Simon whistled the warning from the tree down the road. I jumped out to grab the horse's reins, but it wasn't calm Moses plodding along with Rhoda's cart. It was a centurion's horse and chariot."

The boys gasped, and the women in the other boat tittered.

"The massive horse reared and came down pawing. Malchus and Simon ran away, but I was trampled under the horse's hooves. It happened in seconds; it lasted for years." James shook his head and took a deep breath. "It still hurts to talk about it. My mother cried and wailed. I thought I must be dying. My sister was so pale, and my father." He peered into the fog of a wet and dreary past. "I wasn't sure if he was angrier with me or the doctor. Time left no doubt; he was angry with me.

"I was an invalid. I became a beggar near the temple where a few coins might be tossed my way each day." He looked out over the water. "Malchus and Simon still talked with me sometimes, but their lives went on without me. Later Malchus married Rhoda, and they raised a brood of ten boys, all crazy like their father." He chuckled, then sighed. "I was poor, dependent on others, a nothing. My nephew, Felix, would wheel me to the temple and back home each day."

James looked at little Paul. Behind his watery eyes were a thousand hurts.

"I never asked my nephew to stay or to help me into the healing pool waters. I could tell Felix didn't want to be near me. He never talked to me when he rolled me to the temple in the morning. He would place some bread and a flask of milk in my pocket, then turn tail and run like a rabbit before the other boys ever saw him."

"The nets are heavy," one of the men called out.

Everyone helped haul in the mullet and sea bream. There would be enough for both breakfast and a tidy profit. They sailed for shore.

"If you were lame, how come you walk now?" Paul asked, looking at James but holding onto his father's hand.

"Well, that's a good question. You see, one day I met Jesus."

"You did?"

"On the evening before the Sabbath, Felix would bring me an extra portion of food. I was expected to stay at the temple so that no one would have to carry me. Sometimes I was permitted to stay home for the Sabbath, but more people went to the temple on Saturday, so coins were tossed more often then."

"Oh." Paul nodded.

"So there I sat, chewing on a cheese rind and wincing each time the waters in the pool were stirred. People walked by tossing their coins, but they always kept on walking." James pulled on his lamb's-wool beard and took a deep breath. "But then … then someone stopped. I knew he was staring at me. You get used to it after a while." He shrugged his shoulders, but his voice quivered.

"'How are you today?' the man asked me.

"'Same as always.' I hated being ignored, but hated even more the looks of pity. 'Just sitting here on my golden pallet waiting for the servants to bring me some figs and wine.' My tongue could bite sharper than my teeth." James chomped his rotting teeth at the little boys on the floor of the boat.

Paul covered his mouth with a hand, and Caleb scooted behind his brother.

"'How long have you been like this?' the man asked. "He wasn't giving up on me.

"'A long time,' I answered. 'Are you dropping some money or moving on?'" James looked at the boys. "You'll never guess what he asked then."

"What?" Paul asked as Caleb peeked out from behind him.

"He said, 'Would you like to be healed?'"

"That's crazy!" Paul's eyes bugged out.

James laughed.

"Jesus asked a lot of people that," John said.

"Well, I did want healed, but I figured he was just being cruel. 'Of course I want to be healed. I don't suppose you would like to hang around and help me into the water?'" James looked across the sea toward shore. "I was rude. I had become someone that no one liked, not even myself."

The water splashed as the men rowed toward shore. Caleb reached out to touch one of the shiny fish lying on the boat's deck. It flipped its tail and slithered into the pile of fish caught in the net.

"'Pick up your mat and walk,' he told me. "Simple as saying 'Pick up that fish,' or 'The sun sure is bright.' Ordinary words ... but that was it: 'Pick up your mat and walk.' A prickly feeling started in my toes, and then like the bronze needle the doctor had used, pricks of pain shot fire through my legs. Suddenly I felt a strength and power that I hadn't felt since I was a boy. It was almost involuntary. I bent my legs, and they moved. I jumped from the pallet, scooped up the bed roll, and took off."

One of the men jumped out of the boat and pushed the women's boat the rest of the way to shore. He helped them climb out and then carried Philomena up to the sandy beach.

Two of the younger men helped James and John out of the boat.

Paul waded through the water, but Caleb rode on his father's shoulders. He bounced up and down like a rider on a horse.

The men dragged the heavy net from the boat and sorted the fish in the shallow water.

"You go on with your mother," the boys' father called and turned back to the nets.

The women and children climbed the slope to the fire pit where they had enjoyed the stories at night. Paul helped build up the fire while Caleb ran with the other kids to search for driftwood to burn. It didn't take long before the men returned with skewered fish to cook over the fire.

Caleb pushed into the group of men to sit on the ground near James. He watched as they turned the fish on the long sticks.

"Did you learn to fish from Jesus?" Caleb asked, leaning his pudgy elbow on James's thigh.

James laughed and drew Caleb close. "No, my father taught me to fish long before that. I nearly didn't even follow Jesus. That's what makes my story sad."

"Why?"

"Well," James said, rotating the fish, "after I grabbed my mat, I took off down the corridor, leaping and jumping like a spring lamb."

Caleb giggled.

"But then a Pharisee, dressed for the Sabbath in his robes and phylacteries, stopped me." James lowered his chin to his chest and deepened his voice. "'What are you doing carrying your mat on the Sabbath?' Holier-than-Moses-on-the-mountain dripped from his beard. He grabbed my arm, and I nearly dropped my things."

"That was mean." Caleb balled up his fists and crossed his arms.

"Mm," James agreed. "I told him, 'The man who healed me said to take up my mat and walk. It's not my fault.' I didn't want to get in trouble," he whispered in Caleb's ear.

"Oh." Caleb nodded his head and looked back at the fire.

"But he wouldn't let it go at that. 'What do you mean "healed" you?' he asked. I told him all about how I was hurt and how I sat there waiting for thirty-eight years—"

"Wow, that's older than Papa."

Everyone laughed, and Caleb looked around. His father came over and sat next to them. Caleb hid his face in his father's chest.

"It's a long, long time, that's for sure." James reached over and tousled the boy's hair, then went on, "It didn't seem to matter to the Pharisee. 'Who was this man who healed you?' he wanted to know, but I had been so excited to be able to walk that I took off without ever asking Jesus's name. I stood there with my mouth open, not sure what to say or do. I dropped my bed roll and took off running." James burst out laughing. "It must've been something to see."

"Didn't he yell for you to come back?" Paul asked and sat down near James.

The other children crowded around with him.

Paul and Caleb's father took the long skewer of fish from James. "Maybe you better just tell your story." He smiled at James.

Nodding, James turned around on his knees, swallowed hard, and began. "I was running, not sure if it was running away or running home, but whatever it was, I ran around the corner and who do you suppose I bumped into?" He looked around at all the children.

"Jesus!" Paul yelled.

"Another Pharisee?" a girl asked.

"Your nephew, Felix."

James shook his head and grinned. "No, you're all wrong. It was Malchus and Rhoda."

"Was she in her cart with the horse?" Caleb asked.

"No." James shook his head and smiled at the little boy. "Remember, a long time had gone by. They were bringing their new grandson to the temple for his dedication. Malchus was stunned to see me standing, even running. He just kept saying my name and asking if it was really me. His eyes were as big as a harvest moon.

"I looked at Malchus and Rhoda standing there with their children and their children's children, and I couldn't take it. I realized how much I had missed in life. I was jealous, and probably a little embarrassed." He pursed his lips and lifted his shoulders. "Well, a lot embarrassed. ... Instead of saying anything I took off running another direction. But it had been so long since I had run or done anything very physical, I had to stop and catch my breath.

"I turned another corner and grabbed hold of a cart. I stood there panting like a runaway horse."

James took deep breaths and heaved his shoulders and back to show the kids. They all started mimicking him.

"Then I heard someone laughing from behind me. I turned around to see Jesus, only I didn't know that was his name."

"Ohhhh," the children chorused.

"'So you have skipped walking and gone straight to a marathon, I see,' he said."

The children laughed and pushed at each other.

"A marathon," one of the boys said and snorted.

"It's funny now, but I didn't think so when it happened."

The children quieted as James continued, "In fact it kind of made me mad. 'Who are you and what do you want?' I growled. But Jesus didn't get mad. He said, 'I want to heal your heart. You must forgive the sins of youth and move on with your new life. Stay in the temple and worship the Lord. Sin no more.' And then the crowd engulfed him again as people called out, 'There he is! There's Jesus!'

"That was the last straw. I had heard of him, and I knew the rulers were looking for a way to get rid of him. I made up my mind right then that I would get even for all the years that had been taken from me. It made me mad that he tried to lecture me. I didn't think I was the one who had sinned. It was Malchus and Simon who had left me. They were the sinners. And if that wasn't enough, Malchus had married Rhoda when he knew I always liked her …" James's focus drifted above the circle of children and his voice trailed off.

"But what happened?" Caleb pulled on James's sleeve.

James looked down at the children and cleared his throat. "Well, I did something I'm ashamed of. I went back to that Pharisee and told him Jesus was the one who healed me. He took me into an inner room, one I never would have been allowed into before, and the men there gave me a tray of meats and breads. They asked me everything I knew about Jesus, and then they started plotting together. I could tell they were up to no good, but I didn't care." He bit his lower lip. "Not until it was too late, anyway."

Caleb's dad patted James's shoulder. "It would have happened with or without you. And it wasn't too late, not for you. It's not too late for any of us."

✤ An Ancient Story ✤
(John 5)

At first glance as you read this story in John, you may ask why this healing is a sign. The other gospels list similar healings of paralyzed people, so why does John count this among the signs? The answer seems to lie in the second part of verse 9. It was the Sabbath.

The Sabbath was a holy day for the Jews, a day of rest to honor God. To break Sabbath was beyond sin because it dishonored God.

Jesus said he saw his Father working on the Sabbath (John 5:17). The Father would send rain, allow birth and death, even bless the circumcisions performed on the Sabbath. If God could work on the Sabbath, then surely his Son could do the same.

And now Jesus had really done it. He was calling himself not just a child of God, but *the* child of God, his Son. To the Pharisees this was blasphemy. For John's readers it was a sign of Jesus's authority.

My fictional account of the healing of James focuses on his attitude. Notice in the biblical account that Jesus tells the man to stop sinning or something worse may happen to him.

1. **What could be worse than paralysis for thirty-eight years?**

This warning appears to be about judgment, not physical curses. Later Jesus will heal a blind man and explain that his blindness was not a curse, but was to glorify God. So if this caution to James didn't concern a physical curse, why would Jesus warn about judgment? There must have been something in the man's attitude that needed adjusting.

2. **What about you? Have you experienced some type of healing only to allow your attitude to make you eternally sick? Have you taken to heart Jesus's warning to go and sin no more?**

In Deuteronomy 2, the writer tells us that the Israelites had been wandering for thirty-eight years. Then the original fighting men were dead. They were hopeless.

The invalid in John's story had been disabled for thirty-eight years. He, too, was hopeless. "I have no one to help me into the pool when the water is stirred. While I am trying to get in, someone else goes down ahead of me" (John 5:7 NIV).

I don't know if John meant to connect these two stories with the reference to thirty-eight years, but both stories find the characters without hope, at the end of their rope. The Promised Land looked impossible to the Israelites. Walking again was a pipe dream for the invalid.

Jesus didn't let the man's hopelessness defer the miracle, just as God didn't let the hopeless Israelites wander forever.

God and Jesus are the purveyors of hope.

3. **What situation in your life looks hopeless?**
4. **What if deliverance is two years away, or twenty, or eternity? Will you accept hope even in hopelessness?**

Notice that Jesus was walking near the pool where a "great number of disabled people used to lie" (John 5:3 NIV). He walked among the outcasts, the hurting, sick, lame, diseased. He intentionally went to them. He walked where others dared not tread.

Then in verse 14, Jesus "found" the former invalid at the temple. Jesus made a point of looking for the man.

Jesus will search for you as well. You don't have to be healed already. You don't have to be perfect. You certainly don't have to be sinless.

He is searching for you this instant.

JOHN 5

¹ After this there was a feast of the Jews, and Jesus went up to Jerusalem.

² Now there is in Jerusalem by the Sheep Gate a pool, in Aramaic called Bethesda, which has five roofed colonnades. ³ In these lay a multitude of invalids—blind, lame, and paralyzed. ⁵ One man was there who had been an invalid for thirty-eight years. ⁶ When Jesus saw him lying there and knew that he had already been there a long time, he said to him, "Do you want to be healed?" ⁷ The sick man answered him, "Sir, I have no one to put me into the pool when the water is stirred up, and while I am going another steps down before me." ⁸ Jesus said to him, "Get up, take up your bed, and walk." ⁹ And at once the man was healed, and he took up his bed and walked.

Now that day was the Sabbath. ¹⁰ So the Jews said to the man who had been healed, "It is the Sabbath, and it is not lawful for you to take up your bed." ¹¹ But he answered them, "The man who healed me, that man said to me, 'Take up your bed, and walk.'" [12] They asked him, "Who is the man who said to you, 'Take up your bed and walk'?" [13] Now the man who had been healed did not know who it was, for Jesus had withdrawn, as there was a crowd in the place. [14] Afterward Jesus found him in the temple and said to him, "See, you are well! Sin no more, that nothing worse may happen to you." [15] The man went away and told the Jews that it was Jesus who had healed him. [16] And this was why the Jews were persecuting Jesus, because he was doing these things on the Sabbath. [17] But Jesus answered them, "My Father is working until now, and I am working."

[18] This was why the Jews were seeking all the more to kill him, because not only was he breaking the Sabbath, but he was even calling God his own Father, making himself equal with God.

[19] So Jesus said to them, "Truly, truly, I say to you, the Son can do nothing of his own accord, but only what he sees the Father doing. For whatever the Father does, that the Son does likewise. [20] For the Father loves the Son and shows him all that he himself is doing. And greater works than these will he show him, so that you may marvel. [21] For as the Father raises the dead and gives them life, so also the Son gives life to whom he will. [22] For the Father judges no one, but has given all judgment to the Son, [23] that all may honor the Son, just as they honor the Father. Whoever does not honor the Son does not honor the Father who sent him. [24] Truly, truly, I say to you, whoever hears my word and believes him who sent

me has eternal life. He does not come into judgment, but has passed from death to life.

²⁵ "Truly, truly, I say to you, an hour is coming, and is now here, when the dead will hear the voice of the Son of God, and those who hear will live. ²⁶ For as the Father has life in himself, so he has granted the Son also to have life in himself. ²⁷ And he has given him authority to execute judgment, because he is the Son of Man. ²⁸ Do not marvel at this, for an hour is coming when all who are in the tombs will hear his voice ²⁹ and come out, those who have done good to the resurrection of life, and those who have done evil to the resurrection of judgment.

³⁰ "I can do nothing on my own. As I hear, I judge, and my judgment is just, because I seek not my own will but the will of him who sent me. ³¹ If I alone bear witness about myself, my testimony is not true. ³² There is another who bears witness about me, and I know that the testimony that he bears about me is true. ³³ You sent to John, and he has borne witness to the truth. ³⁴ Not that the testimony that I receive is from man, but I say these things so that you may be saved. ³⁵ He was a burning and shining lamp, and you were willing to rejoice for a while in his light. ³⁶ But the testimony that I have is greater than that of John. For the works that the Father has given me to accomplish, the very works that I am doing, bear witness about me that the Father has sent me. ³⁷ And the Father who sent me has himself borne witness about me. His voice you have never heard, his form you have never seen, ³⁸ and you do not have his word abiding in you, for you do not believe the one whom he has sent. ³⁹ You

search the Scriptures because you think that in them you have eternal life; and it is they that bear witness about me, [40] yet you refuse to come to me that you may have life. [41] I do not receive glory from people. [42] But I know that you do not have the love of God within you. [43] I have come in my Father's name, and you do not receive me. If another comes in his own name, you will receive him. [44] How can you believe, when you receive glory from one another and do not seek the glory that comes from the only God? [45] Do not think that I will accuse you to the Father. There is one who accuses you: Moses, on whom you have set your hope. [46] For if you believed Moses, you would believe me; for he wrote of me. [47] But if you do not believe his writings, how will you believe my words?"

✥ A MODERN STORY ✥

Some tears taste like birthday cake, sweet and celebratory. Some tears contain a hint of meringue, lightness that melts on your cheeks. Other tears are hot and heavy, like biscuits and gravy; they leave you full and comforted. And then there are painful tears, sharp vinegar biting all the way down.

She was only a child, but vinegar was all she had ever tasted. Demetra was five or six years old when her mother died; time was a mystery to her. Her mother was an alcoholic who died in a car accident.

Her new adoptive home was pretty on the outside, but ugly on the inside. A childless couple in rural North Carolina adopted young Demetra along with a little boy. The woman, Mama, loved her children, but Daddy was another story. He was mean and abusive. He practiced witchcraft and sorcery. By age thirteen Demetra had seen enough.

She began running away to friends' houses. Mama would hunt her down, threaten her friends with police reports, and then drag Demetra back home. When Demetra confided to her Aunt Bessie what was going on in the house, Bessie was livid. She couldn't believe her own brother would be so cruel. Demetra was placed into Social Services' custody.

She bounced around from one girls' home to another. She started drinking, and became violent and destructive. The story never changed, only the characters and setting. Demetra suffered beatings, rapes, forced consumption of bodily wastes, and hatred. By fifteen she was pregnant and had nowhere to turn. She went back home, this time to stay with a different aunt.

Mama had taught her about church and prayer. She had made certain that Demetra knew there was a higher power. *Perhaps*, Demetra thought, *it will be different this time*. It was not.

The abuse continued at home. She left her baby and escaped to the arms of various men. Some only wanted to hurt her, but others were helpful. One was a teacher who arranged for her to be part of a program that would help her get a job and finish high school. She started working as an aide with troubled teens, but it was too much temptation. She began drinking more heavily and drugs entered her life.

Other men rescued her from the streets only to abuse her in private. She had two more children, both lost to her until years later. She tried working for restaurants, stores in the mall, but with no diploma and no residence, she was overlooked and under-loved. The beaten, young woman didn't know she was an alcoholic; she only knew that drinking eased her emotions and helped her forget. Acrid, smoke-filled tears choked and burned her. There was no taste, nothing to fill her, nothing to offer sustenance.

Finally Demetra was imprisoned. But it was in prison that she remembered what Aunt Bessie had told her years ago: "Always know that there's a God, and he loves you."

Demetra suffered a stroke the night she was placed in that cell. Help was slow in coming, but in the prison infirmary she met an angel. The nurse there bathed her and cared for her. She told her that God had a calling on her life. There was a reason she was still alive.

When at last she was released from prison, the now middle-aged Demetra found herself in another promiscuous and abusive relationship. She escaped to a domestic abuse shelter. There she found people who believed she was worth saving, worth loving. They saw an abandoned child who needed rescuing. They dried her tears and washed her face.

Demetra began attending church. She joined Alcoholics Anonymous. She went back to school and completed her high school education. She received job training, found work, got married. With the help of her support system Demetra even finished college! She was reunited with her children and met her granddaughter. Finally she tasted sweet-tea tears of refreshment.

Demetra's life has changed. She knows real love, understands happiness and acceptance, comprehends what it means to be part of a family and a community. The biggest change in Demetra's life is that she knows Jesus. She has felt his miraculous touch.

It didn't happen overnight. It was not the type of healing that stuns and causes people to gawk, but slowly over time, Demetra has been healed—is being healed.

Demetra says that she gets angry sometimes and she feels worried a lot, but then she remembers what Aunt Bessie taught her so long ago: God loves her. She thinks about the times that God was all she had, and that he was enough. He really was all she needed.

Demetra says she wants the faith and strength of Job. She bows her head and stares at her hands. "But the little bit of faith and strength I have is enough to fight Satan, now that I know who I'm really fighting."

The Sovereign Lord will wipe away the tears from all faces; he will remove his people's disgrace from all the earth. The Lord has spoken. (Isaiah 25:8 NIV)[1]

✤ REFLECTION ✤

Everyone has a choice to make. The lame man in John 5 chose to report Jesus to the authorities. He may not have known what would happen. He might have had good intentions in pointing Jesus out. The other three gospels tell another story, a woman's story (Matthew 9, Mark 5, Luke 8) that can only be interpreted as the choice of faith and trust. I imagine it like this:

Meanwhile, Jesus moved on with the crowd. They were laughing and bumping into each other, sweating under

---

1   This section is based on material from the following source: Demetra Campbell, interview by Traci L. Stead, Aug. 26, 2017.

the noonday sun. Stopping for a drink, Jesus was jostled by the crowd.

"Who touched me?" Jesus asked.

"In this crowd, you want to know who touched you?" Peter laughed.

But Jesus wouldn't let it be. Glancing around the throng, his eyes fell on Susannah. She was hiding beneath her head dressing, but her frightened eyes dodged up to the man standing in front of them all. Like a deer entering the evening meadow, Susannah stepped forward.

"It was me," she whispered. "I touched your cloak."

The crowd hushed. Peter and Thomas grabbed hold of her arms to see what Jesus would do to this forward woman. But Jesus only asked why she had touched him. The gentleness in his voice gave her the courage to speak further.

"My husband and I want to have a baby, but the children always die before they can see the sun," Susannah explained. "Finally the last child was too much for me. I'm unclean. I've hemorrhaged for twelve years now. My husband is kind, but I know he wants a son. I've spent all my money on doctor's bills and advice, but nothing helps. I thought if I just touched your cloak, surely such a holy man could heal me." Tears dripped from her chin. "As soon as I touched your robe, I knew I was better. My whole body was strong and healthy. I stole your power; I'm sorry. Please, forgive me." Susannah fell to her knees.

"Dear woman," Jesus said. "It's not my power but your faith that has healed you. Go in peace."

Both James and Susannah received healing from Jesus, but they responded very differently. One turned Jesus over to the authorities; the other turned herself over to Jesus.

1. **What have you decided to do with Jesus? Are you giving in to bitterness and despair, or are you searching for the healing that Jesus offers?**

Time was a factor for James and Susannah, and still is for Demetra. The man in the scriptures was an invalid for thirty-eight years, the woman suffered for twelve, and Demetra has been fighting demons for forty years at least. What seems to us a ridiculously long time, though, is only a breath to God. His timing is not ours.

I don't know why people suffer for so long. I don't know why an all-powerful God doesn't just snap his fingers and solve everything. In Daniel 10, an angel visited the prophet Daniel. He told Daniel that he was highly respected, and that God had heard him three weeks ago when he humbled himself, but the angel was delayed in coming because of another fight going on in Persia. There were other things to attend to before Daniel could be helped.

In some ways this story gives me hope—God listens and acts, but my situation may not be as dire as I believe. There are other stories in which God acts instantly and without reserve, so if the story in Daniel is to be an example, God will send help when it is needed.

2. **What long-time struggle are you dealing with? Are you counting years, like the invalid and the woman?**
3. **Do you feel certain that Jesus will offer healing when the time is right?**

John wrote to confirm that Jesus is the Messiah. The healing of the invalid is the third sign. It is here that Jesus began to confront the traditions of the Pharisees. He healed on the Sabbath. The confrontation began with the now whole man. He was carrying his mat and walking through the temple. The Pharisees chastised him, and the man explained that he was just healed, and the healer told him to carry his mat.

This resulted in a hunt for Jesus. Jesus's defense was "My Father is always at work to this very day, and I too am working" (John 5:17 NIV). Now he'd done it. Not only was Jesus breaking Sabbath rules, but he was claiming equality with God by being his Son.

Jesus went on to explain that the Son only does what the Father does. He said if they really knew the Father and the scriptures, they would recognize that he was the Son.

4. **What scriptures do you know that identify Jesus as the Son of God?**

The confrontation in John 5 ends in a problem still relevant in today's world. Jesus came in the name of God, but the Pharisees didn't accept him. He asserted that if someone came in their own name, the Pharisees would have gladly accepted that person. He said that they wanted pats on the back from each other but weren't all that concerned about God's praise.

Our lives are filled with hashtags, bylines, thumbs-up, emoticons, and shout-outs. I am the first to admit that when I mow the grass, I expect my husband to gush over how good that lawn looks. I check my Instagram account to see how many likes I get on a picture and then wonder why there aren't more hearts. I'm pleased when someone notices the extra effort I give a project, and hurt and angry when I don't get positive feedback.

Jesus equates this behavior with not having the love of God in our hearts. Astonishing. Shocking. In John 12:42-43, John says that many of the leaders did believe in Jesus, but they would not tell others because they "loved human praise more than praise from God" (NIV).

It isn't wrong to receive praise from others. Praise is a blessing and an encouragement to us. The problem is when we refuse to give glory to Jesus because we want the praise of people.

5.   **What does "praise from God" sound like? Have you ever experienced it?**

✤ ACTION ✤

1.   All of us have gone through times of suffering. If you are old enough to read this book, you have suffered. No one's pain is less important than another's. We often acknowledge pain in levels: a divorce is worse than a job loss but not worse than two children dying. Poppycock. Pain hurts and no one's pain is less meaningful than someone else's. The important thing is how we react to pain and suffering. Do we allow pain to bring us closer to God, or do we, like the crippled man in John, turn Jesus over to his enemies? Evaluate your response to suffering, then meditate on Psalm 73.

2.   Job is the epitome of suffering, and his friends came to offer their condolences. They may not have had

the best advice, they may not have believed that Job was righteous, they may not even have believed that God loved Job. But they came to sit with their friend, to be with him, to share in his pain. Make a list of your friends who are right now suffering—perhaps an illness, the death of a loved one, a prodigal child—and then reach out to them. Call and talk. Go out for coffee. Send a card. Invite them to your home. Share the love of God and the warmth of a human hand.

3. None of us wants to suffer alone. God is with us, but we are also with others. If you're doing this study as a group, gather together and go minister to the hurting this week. Take a meal to a family, go to a hospitality house at the hospital, serve at the homeless shelter. Go in the name of Jesus and offer his comfort.

CHAPTER 5

HE FEEDS

✤ A REUNION ✤

"Times like these always remind me of when I met Jesus."
A man looked across the harbor at the boats headed out for night
fishing. He shaded his eyes from the rays glinting off the water.

The evening sun warmed Caleb's back as he waited on
the ground with the children. The men sat on the benches,
and the women filled plates from a makeshift table of planks
and benches.

"Speak up," said Caleb's father.

"It was spring, and I was just a boy. My mother gave me
permission to climb the mountains and listen to the teacher. The
planting was done, and we kids weren't needed just then."

Caleb watched the man talking. His tanned skin and
wrinkled face looked like his own father's.

"That's my papa," a little girl whispered nearby. She sat up on
her knees and listened.

Caleb followed suit.

"It was getting close to the Festival, I remember, and a lot of people were talking about Jesus. Some people thought he was amazing, healing people and all, but others were angry and fearful. Those were the ones who stayed in town." The man looked around at everyone. He took another bite of fish and washed it down with some water. "I wasn't sure what I thought. I heard my parents talking sometimes, but they weren't very political. They just wanted what we all want, I suppose—to be healthy and safe." He shrugged his shoulders.

"Anyway, Mother said I could go see what it was all about, so she packed me a little lunch and I took off for the hills. Can't say I paid too much attention to the teacher, really. I was having fun being with the crowd, hiking in the spring air and green grass, sleeping under the stars. It was fun." He laughed.

"But it wasn't all fun and games," John's voice interrupted. "I remember a lot of anger and tension. People wanted Jesus to do more, show more power. They didn't understand what he was all about."

"You're right." The man nodded his head. "I was young, though; that didn't worry me. I just wanted to see what all the fuss was about, maybe witness a miracle." He chuckled. "Little did I know I was about to be part of a miracle."

Caleb reached up for the plate his mother was passing. Olives rolled across his chubby fingers.

"Careful," his mother whispered as she sat down behind him.

"Most everyone had arrived on the plain. The shepherds were irritated because so many people were trampling the grass. I guess there were at least five thousand men; I heard someone say that.

"Some other boys and I were throwing rocks to see who could throw farthest when one of Jesus's disciples came around asking if anyone had food to share with Jesus. 'I've got five loaves and two fish,' I spoke up. Andrew—that was the disciple—took me through the crowd to Jesus."

"Was he nice?" Caleb asked, licking his wet fingers.

"Shh," his mother said and nudged his backside with her toe.

The man smiled. "Yes, he was nice. Very nice indeed. Andrew asked if he could take my basket to share with everyone. I just nodded, figuring he meant with the men around Jesus." He waved his arm around the table.

The men there grunted in agreement.

"But Andrew and all the others had everyone … everyone … sit down on the grass in groups. Then Jesus prayed and started handing out the bread and fish. They brought it around to us in hand baskets. John was there. Tell them."

John licked the fish from his fingers and took a drink of water. "Twelve. That's how many disciples were in the inner circle. … And that's how many baskets we filled with leftovers from Micah's little lunch. It didn't sink in right away, what he had done. There wasn't time, really. The people were going crazy, talking about making Jesus king. Jesus headed up onto the mountain and told us to keep talking with the people. We stayed 'til nearly dark, then everyone headed out to make camp or find lodging in town. We got a boat and headed to Capernaum. I remember being so tired."

"Yes, I was tired too." The younger man picked the story back up. "I slept out in the field with the shepherds. I'd filled my little lunch basket with some of the fish and bread, and I ate that the next day when I walked back home. I heard people talking about chasing Jesus down, but my mother wouldn't have let me go so far across the lake." He shrugged and tore off a piece of bread.

A grin crossed his face as he handed it down to Caleb. "Always listen to your mother."

✠ AN ANCIENT STORY ✠
(JOHN 6:1-15)

John 6:1-13 (NIV) offers a glimpse of Jesus's extravagance. The vocabulary John used is lush: "a great crowd" … "plenty of grass" … "as much as they wanted" … "they all had enough to eat" … "filled twelve baskets." Notice that they were in the middle of nowhere, but a great crowd was following him up the mountain. It was spring, nearly time for the annual Passover Festival. Instead of heading to Jerusalem, people were heading to Jesus. He seated them on soft grass and more than filled their bellies. Their response? They intended to make him king by force.

1. Have you ever taken advantage of Jesus's extravagance and tried to "force" him to do things your way? How did that go?
2. How did Jesus react to the people on the mountain?
3. Jesus singled out Philip for the test. What has Jesus asked you lately?
4. Was your response disbelief and incredulity, as Philip's was? Or did you, like Andrew, find an impossible solution to show Jesus just how ridiculous the situation was?

Jesus often went up on mountains during his ministry. He gave sermons and taught from mountains, healed on mountains, and was transfigured on a mountain. It was on Mount Olivet that he cried out to the Father and on the mount of Golgotha that he gave his life.

Mountains are symbolic of the divine throughout history. On Mount Ararat, Noah and his family exited the ark and entered a new Eden. Mount Moriah was the testing ground for the patriarch Abraham as he planned to sacrifice his son. Moses climbed Mount Pisgah to glimpse the Promised Land. Elijah called down fire on Mount Carmel.

On Mount Sinai, God gave the Ten Commandments to Moses. The mountain was covered with smoke and thunder rolled. The people feared for their lives. In fact the Israelites asked if they could stay home instead of going on the mountain with Moses.

But on the mountainside John tells us about—the barren hillsides east of the lake across from the city of Tiberias—the people didn't fear. They climbed the mountain with eager expectation. They went for healing and encouraging words. They got all that and more besides.

5.   **Where do you go to chase down Jesus?**

In John 6:12, the NIV translates Jesus as saying, "Gather the pieces that are left over. Let nothing be wasted." A more common translation, and perhaps more accurate to the intention of John, is "that nothing may be lost."

In 6:39, Jesus said that the will of God is that Jesus should lose none of the people he has been given. Chapter 6 is best read in its entirety to understand what John was trying to do, but for this study I will tell you that John explained the Lord's Supper in a symbolic teaching in the synagogue of Capernaum. John began with the feeding of the five thousand

and ended with the teaching on bread from heaven and eating Jesus's flesh.

What exactly did Jesus mean that twelve baskets were gathered so that none would be lost? Was he talking about food, disciples, or future followers? It might have been a lesson for the disciples as each one gathered a basket of leftovers, or perhaps it was a symbolic gathering of the twelve tribes of Israel. Whatever it was, it was done so that none would be lost.

6. **What hard teaching are you struggling with? Is it causing you to leave, or are you gathered into a basket with all the other questioners waiting for the answers?**

7. **What sign will convince you that Jesus is the Savior?**

JOHN 6:1-15

[1] After this Jesus went away to the other side of the Sea of Galilee, which is the Sea of Tiberias. [2] And a large crowd was following him, because they saw the signs that he was doing on the sick. [3] Jesus went up on the mountain, and there he sat down with his disciples. [4] Now the Passover, the feast of the Jews, was at hand. [5] Lifting up his eyes, then, and seeing that a large crowd was coming toward him, Jesus said to Philip, "Where are we to buy bread, so that these people may eat?" [6] He said this to test him, for he himself knew what he would do. [7] Philip answered him, "Two hundred denarii worth of bread would not be enough for each of them to get a little." [8] One of his disciples, Andrew, Simon Peter's brother, said to him, [9] "There is a boy here who has five barley loaves and two fish, but what are they for so

many?" ¹⁰ Jesus said, "Have the people sit down." Now there was much grass in the place. So the men sat down, about five thousand in number. ¹¹ Jesus then took the loaves, and when he had given thanks, he distributed them to those who were seated. So also the fish, as much as they wanted. ¹² And when they had eaten their fill, he told his disciples, "Gather up the leftover fragments, that nothing may be lost." ¹³ So they gathered them up and filled twelve baskets with fragments from the five barley loaves left by those who had eaten. ¹⁴ When the people saw the sign that he had done, they said, "This is indeed the Prophet who is to come into the world!"

¹⁵ Perceiving then that they were about to come and take him by force to make him king, Jesus withdrew again to the mountain by himself.

✤ A MODERN STORY ✤

Money never miraculously multiplied for George Müller before he met Jesus. His father was a tax collector in Prussia in the early 1800s. According to George his father entrusted the children with more than he should have for ones so young. Before he was ten years old, George began lying, cheating, and stealing to get more money. By the time he was sixteen, he was jailed as a thief and a vagabond. His father sent him to seminary to become a clergyman, but George spent the money on expensive hotels and food. When it was gone, he went back home to get more.

About a year later George decided to take his father's advice and went to seminary again. He studied hard and impressed his teachers, though he cared nothing for God. He had over three hundred books, but didn't own a single Bible. When George was twenty, he and some other seminarians took loans against their schoolbooks and set out to travel Prussia and Switzerland. George was a modern Judas, keeping the moneybag and making sure his trip didn't cost as much as everyone else's. He was still a thief.

But then George encountered Jesus in a small house church.

A friend invited George to attend a gathering of believers. Singing, praying, and listening to a printed sermon were the planned activities. As the small group of Christians kneeled to pray, George heard the first earnest prayer of his life. It was a prayer not for self, but to spread God's work and love to others. George's life changed.

Over the next couple of years George devoted himself to Bible study and preaching the Word. He was interested in missions and applied to be a missionary in Bucharest. War between the Turks and Russians stopped George from going, but he was sure that God wanted him to be a missionary.

As George looked for missions opportunities, he turned back to his gambling ways. Instead of waiting for God to tell him what to do, George cast lots for answers. After several of these situations went poorly, George learned that he had to wait for God to answer, and the waiting had to be in fervent prayer.

One of the first things George waited for was a wife. God didn't drag his feet; George and Mary were united in 1830. Mary agreed that prayer should hold the utmost importance in their relationship, and they should trust God for all their needs. It would be the biggest gamble of his life, but the odds were the best he could ever imagine.

As time passed, George and Mary served in a small congregation in England. They didn't take a salary but relied completely on the Lord for their daily needs. God did not fail them.

In 1832, George and Mary moved to Bristol, England, to begin a ministry there. Many times the Müllers had no food or money in the house, but by the end of the day God always provided. At the end of 1833, George tallied up God's blessings to approximately $3,700. If he had accepted a salary from the church, it would have been $900. George was beginning to see that God is the Great Provider—of both blessings and needs.

George also started feeling concern for the orphaned children on the streets of Bristol. So the extra money that came in was spent on the children. He brought them into his home each morning, fed them, and taught them scriptures. Older people also joined these morning feasts until George and Mary were feeding thirty to forty people each morning. As the numbers increased, so did God's blessings.

George and his ministry partner, Henry Craik, founded the Scriptural Knowledge Institute to expand the reach of the gospel. They pledged to buy Bibles and Christian tracts as well as support orphans. They would not ask for money from anyone, but they would pray and ask God to provide what was needed.

At the end of 1835, George felt led to ask God for a place to house orphans. He asked God for 1,000 pounds and the right people to run the house. In April 1836, the first orphan house opened, only five months after he began praying. He had not asked a single person for money.

In October the same year the Müllers opened a second house in Bristol. One day in 1837, they had no food in the house for the children. George had the staff and children set the table as usual and went to the Father in prayer for their daily bread. A knock sounded at the door. The town baker stood at the door with loaves of fresh bread. He said God had awakened him in the middle of the night and told him to bake for the orphans. As the baker left, the milkman stopped outside the house. A wheel had broken on his cart and the milk would be stolen if he left it on the cart while he went to fix the wheel. He offered the milk to the orphan house. The children sat down to breakfast, eating until fully satisfied.

The ministry continued to grow, funded only through prayer. At first the orphanages were rented properties, but as the ministry grew, it became apparent that new living quarters were needed. In 1849, the first Müller-built house, fully funded by prayer, was opened. It housed three hundred orphans. By 1870, there were five houses boarding over two thousand orphans. During the nineteenth century Müller cared for over ten thousand orphans in Bristol.

The ministry continued to grow, and prayer continued to be the only source of fundraising. George Müller passed away in 1898, but his orphan homes did not. The Scriptural Knowledge Institute continued to flourish, serving orphans, elderly, and unchurched peoples around the world. The name of the institute changed over the years until in 2009 it became The George Müller Charitable Trust.

Müllers, as it is best known, continues to serve George's vision. Though orphans and the elderly of Bristol are still the focus, monies have been sent to over forty countries around the world. The trust helps fund clean water, small-business loans, education, and more. Funds are still provided by asking God alone.

George Müller fully collected on Psalm 81:10 (NIV): "I am the Lord your God, who brought you up out of Egypt. Open wide your mouth and I will fill it."[1]

✤ Reflection ✤

It was like a Gregorian chant lisped by kindergarten children:

"God is great. God is good. And we thank him for our food. By his hands we all are fed. Give us, Lord, our daily bread. Amen."

I still smell yeast rolls whenever I sing this prayer. I was five years old standing in line at a public school. We sang our little prayer and then traipsed down the asbestos-tile floor to the school cafeteria. That was back in the day when school food was made from scratch.

It's easy in this time of plenty to forget where our daily bread comes from. I can only think of three restaurants in the town I grew up in. If we were lucky, one Sunday a month we ate open-faced turkey sandwiches at the nice family restaurant. Occasionally we were treated to chili dogs and fresh-cut fries at one of the other places. In the summer we made it a couple of times for an ice cream treat at the summer-only ice cream stop. My current hometown offers well over a hundred restaurant choices, and we frequent them at least once a week. Japanese,

---

1   This section is based on material from the following sources:
    Bonnie Harvey, George Müller: Man of Faith (Uhrichsville, Ohio: Barbour Books, 1998).
    The George Müller Charitable Trust, accessed September 2017, mullers.org.

Chinese, Mexican, Italian, Mediterranean, American—whatever my taste for that day, I can have it.

I order clothes online, books are one click away, and the doctor's office is a few miles down the road. I can talk to my mom whenever and wherever with my cell phone. I can find the answer to any question by asking the same phone. I really don't need anything.

How easy it is to forget that I do have needs. Food, water, clothing, and shelter are still my basic needs, yet I don't recognize them so much when I can turn up the thermostat, pull a steak out of the freezer, or flip on the faucet.

I still thank God. I still pray. But I'm not so sure I still *depend*.

1. **What about you? Do you thank God before breakfast, but know that lunch is as close as a card swipe away? Do you return from a grocery run to stuff more food into an overflowing pantry?**
2. **What bread and fish has Jesus multiplied in your life?**

We were down to $75. Matt had spent the year writing his dissertation. We had two small children and lived with his parents. Though he had searched for a job during that year, none had been offered. It was a year of frustration, depression, and exasperation.

I remember asking a friend to pray for the situation because I couldn't any longer. I was so tired. I knew that God promised to provide, but I wasn't getting the answer I wanted. I wasn't sure if I was following God's will. I wasn't sure if I could believe anymore.

I stopped pleading, stopped begging, stopped going to God in tears. I stopped praying for three months. Oh, I whispered a prayer every now and then, but I just couldn't do it with the regularity I knew it deserved. My friend checked in with me and reassured me she was still entering the throne room on my behalf.

Finally I felt refreshed. It was time to begin praying again.

I don't know how long it was after that until the job came. I'm not sure that it matters. What is important to me is that I returned to the one who could give the blessing. I handed Jesus my crumbly bread and stinky fish, and he filled my basket to overflowing.

3. **Have you reached the bottom of the barrel? Are you tired and frustrated?**

4. **You can acknowledge your dependence on God, but still ask a friend to walk along beside you. Who is that friend in your life?**

When you are able, return to the Father who will provide whatever you need.

———

When the job came we worked for a campus ministry that fed students every Friday. We never knew how many would show up for the free meal. Church groups provided the food, and I cooked some as well. I loved watching the long line of students form as the lunch hour neared.

I dished out soup, lasagna, brisket, whatever the menu was for the day. The line wrapped around the building, and I couldn't see where it ended. I kept on spooning out food; students kept coming around the corner. Not once did we run out of food. Not once.

Hattie Mae Wiatt had 57 cents. She used it to build a hospital and a university. Hattie Mae lived in Philadelphia in the late 1800s. She wanted to go to Sunday school, but the church was too crowded. The preacher told her they needed money to build a bigger church so that all the children could attend. Hattie Mae gave all she had, but she died before anything could be built. She never saw the new church or heard of the fund eventually named for her. The preacher told others what the little girl had done, and the money started growing. If a little girl was willing to give all she had so others could learn about Jesus, then they could give too. Eventually the Wiatt Mite Society would develop Temple University and Hospital. Her money is still multiplying today.[2]

The little boy that Andrew found that day had no idea that his fish and loaves could be multiplied to thousands. But Jesus knew. They were a mustard seed that held a flock of birds (Matthew 13, Luke 13). They were a mountain thrown into the sea (Mark 11, Matthew 21). They were lilies of the field growing into linen robes (Matthew 6, Luke 12).

God really is the Great Provider. He really can multiply whatever little bit you offer. He can even provide bread and milk out of thin air.

All he needs is to hear your prayer.

5. **What is worrying you right now? Are you praying about it?**

---

2   Russell H. Conwell, "The History of Fifty-Seven Cents," Temple University Libraries, accessed January 2018, library.temple.edu/collections/scrc/hattie.

✤ ACTION ✤

1. Look in your wallet. If you are like me, there's a debit card and a handful of change. I don't deal in cash anymore. Take out that handful of bread and fish and see how far it will go. What can you do with that little bit? Buy a postage stamp for a card already stashed away and send an old-fashioned letter to fill someone's heart. Buy a popsicle for a kid at a convenience store. Visit with the child's mother while he eats it. Hide the money and let the local neighborhood kids have a scavenger hunt for it.

2. Start praying for your needs to be filled. God's providence will always surprise you. When our boys were very little, we needed a lamp for their bedroom that would let me get one or the other out of the room without turning on the room lights. We were pinching pennies thinner than paper and a lamp was not in the budget. I started praying, and a week or two later, a woman at church brought me a lamp. She was cleaning out her apartment and just "thought" I might like it for our apartment. It was perfect. But don't just be a taker. Ask God how you can be the answer to someone else's prayer.

3. Join with your Bible study group, neighborhood service organization, or whatever buddies you like to serve with and pull your resources to feed the hungry or help the distraught. Pack lunches for the homeless,

serve at the soup kitchen, hang scarves on a park fence, buy shoes for a poor district school, buy lice shampoo for a school nurse to discreetly put in a school bag, supply the shelter with feminine hygiene products. Like Andrew, look for a way to fill the needs; Jesus will supply the miracle.

CHAPTER 6

HE RESCUES

✢ A REUNION ✢

The fish bones lay in a pile on the makeshift table. The smallest children ran at the edge of the water, shrieking as the waves lapped at their toes. A few of the older boys had walked out on a sandbar and were skimming up minnows for fun. The sun sank lower in the sky. The dusky air felt heavy; the dew would soon fall.

"Tell us a story, John," one of the men said, stretching his arms over his head and then flinging himself onto the sandy ground.

"Yes, yes." Several other men urged John to share.

John smiled and watched the silhouettes playing along the shore. "I can continue the story of the fishes and loaves if you like. My mother didn't make me stay home." He winked at Micah, and John's thin cheeks lifted in a smirk.

Micah smiled and spread his arms in front of himself. "By all means."

John sat in silence for several minutes, waiting for the men to find soft spots and the women to finish clearing the table.

Finally he looked around at the group, closed his eyes, and breathed in the fresh air. "This is just about right. We were in one of Peter's fishing boats sprawled on the floor after the long day. We argued about whose turn it was to sleep or row. Seems like Peter took the helm."

John opened his eyes, staring off across the waves and the distant years. Some gulls swooped down over small crumbs the children had gathered from the bones and bread of dinner.

"The afternoon winds had been mild for a change, and we were looking forward to an uneventful crossing. It was getting past dusk. Most people had gone by then, and we were headed across the water toward Capernaum. Jesus was still up on the mountainside—praying, we supposed."

He faced the listeners. "We'd been on the water a little while when the wind started picking up. Peter called for everyone to help. I joined James at the oar and rowed, but it was a mighty struggle. We were past time for the usual afternoon storms. I don't know where that wind came from, just up out of nowhere.

"I tried not to worry 'til I saw Andrew and Peter struggling to pull the sail. I've weathered my share of storms on the Sea of Galilee, and let me tell you, this was a drowner."

Caleb ran up the shore and fell into his father's lap, sand flying from his feet.

"Is it another story?" he whispered as he stretched his arms up and behind him to circle his father's neck.

His father nodded and patted Caleb's stomach to quiet him.

"I don't know how long we pulled at the ship trying to make it head west. The more we rowed, the farther east we blew. Water was washing over the sides. We were bailing fast, but the waves were faster. Some were nine feet high by my measure.

"We bailed and rowed and prayed, but the winds kept lashing us and the water kept washing us." John paused and looked across the water, narrowing his eyes at the sun glinting off the quiet bay of the Great Sea. "You can't tell when a storm is going to come up like that, but at night …" He shook his head. "Some said a witch cursed us; others—well, our faith wasn't what it should have been."

John rubbed his face and grinned. "We all have our weak moments. I was wishing my mother had made me stay home." He laughed and looked at Micah in the deepening shadows. "Then some cried out that something was coming toward us. It was nearing dawn and a light was glimmering in the east. Turns out it wasn't the sun rising, but the Son walking.

"I think Andrew was the first to see him. I remember him pointing off the stern. 'It's a ghost!' he yelled, and then we all jumped to our feet."

Caleb turned on his father's lap and snuggled tight into him.

"The wind was against us, so the voice was hard to make out, but we could tell the apparition was calling to us. One moment we could see a shape on the water; the next it was swept from sight by the crest of a wave. We were soaked through, but it wasn't dampness that made us shiver. The ghost kept walking closer toward us.

"'It's me—Jesus.' We heard it, but we didn't believe it. How could he be walking on the water? It had to be a ghost. Then Peter—" John snorted and shook his head. "Peter yelled back, 'If it's really you, let me come to you.' I still don't know what possessed him to do that, but Jesus said to come on out."

The men and women gasped. Caleb grabbed his father's hand and covered his eyes. His mother sat down beside them on the sand and gently rubbed his back.

"Peter swung his leg over the side just as a wave crashed over him. He wiped his face and stepped out. I've always admired him for that.

"He got several steps, I suppose, far enough out that we all just stood with our mouths wide open. Then another wave, probably ten or eleven feet high, started toward us. Peter glanced back at us ... and then sank like a rock.

"Jesus ran over to him and jerked him up from the water. They both climbed into the boat and the storm quieted down. Pfft. Just like that." John waved dismissal. "We were all quiet the rest of the way to Capernaum. No one dared say a word."

✦ AN ANCIENT STORY ✦
(JOHN 6:16-71)

John's account of Jesus walking on the water is hardly noticeable. Squeezed between two other stories, its five short verses are easily overlooked. If you are unfamiliar with the story, you might like to look at Matthew 14 or Mark 6.

John's focus is on the Jews' reaction after they found Jesus on the other side of the Sea of Galilee. The story of him walking on the water is mostly a means of explaining their confusion.

Notice the many reactions to Jesus in today's reading: the disciples are frightened, the masses are curious, the Jews are disgruntled, and Peter is confident—at least for a few moments.

1. **What reaction do you have to Jesus during times of storm or during times of difficult teachings?**

The NIV translates Jesus's words in verse 20 as "It is I" because it is difficult in English to make a grammatically correct statement as "I am, don't be afraid." Yet "I am" is what Jesus said. John writes a lot of "I am" statements: I am the bread of life, the light of the world, the gate. I am the vine, the good shepherd, the resurrection and the life. I am the way, the truth, and the life.

God told Moses that his name is "I AM" (Exodus 3:14). John's purpose is to help us believe that Jesus is the Messiah, the Son of God. When Jesus walks on water and declares, "I am," he is saying, I am the Creator who has authority over the wind and the waves.

When the disciples heard Jesus say, "I am" and not to be afraid, they immediately took him into the boat.

2. **How quickly do you accept the Holy One into your own boat? If you haven't let him in, what will it take?**

After Jesus rose from the dead, he explained through scripture that he is the Christ and everything about him that had been foretold. Perhaps Psalm 107 was one of the scriptures he showed them:

> Some went out on the sea in ships; they were merchants on the mighty waters. They saw the works of the LORD, his wonderful deeds in the deep. For he spoke and stirred up a tempest that lifted high the waves. They mounted up to the heavens and went down to the depths; in their peril their courage melted away. They reeled and staggered like drunkards; they were at their wits' end. Then they cried out to the LORD in their trouble, and he brought them out of their distress. He stilled the

storm to a whisper; the waves of the sea were hushed. They were glad when it grew calm, and he guided them to their desired haven. Let them give thanks to the LORD for his unfailing love and his wonderful deeds for mankind. Let them exalt him in the assembly of the people and praise him in the council of the elders. (Psalm 107:23-32 NIV)

The seas are nothing new to God's story. During creation God separated the waters from the heavens and the land (Genesis 1:9-10). Moses led the Israelites on dry ground through the Red Sea (Exodus 14). And the ground was dry again when Joshua led them across the Jordan river bed (Joshua 3). Jonah tried to run from God, was thrown into the sea, and saved by a whale (Jonah 1-2). Paul and Luke survived a terrible storm at sea and were shipwrecked on Malta (Acts 27-28). Each of these stories displays God's power over creation. He alone has authority to command nature.

This mighty power must be frightening to witness, yet Jesus said, "Don't be afraid." When God's angels encountered people, they began with, *"Do not be afraid."* God understands that his supernatural abilities can be unsettling to us.

3. **What miracles have you witnessed that caused you fear or astonishment?**

JOHN 6:16-71

16 When evening came, his disciples went down to the sea, 17 got into a boat, and started across the sea to Capernaum. It was now dark, and Jesus had not yet come

to them. ¹⁸ The sea became rough because a strong wind was blowing. ¹⁹ When they had rowed about three or four miles, they saw Jesus walking on the sea and coming near the boat, and they were frightened. ²⁰ But he said to them, "It is I; do not be afraid." ²¹ Then they were glad to take him into the boat, and immediately the boat was at the land to which they were going.

²² On the next day the crowd that remained on the other side of the sea saw that there had been only one boat there, and that Jesus had not entered the boat with his disciples, but that his disciples had gone away alone. ²³ Other boats from Tiberias came near the place where they had eaten the bread after the Lord had given thanks. ²⁴ So when the crowd saw that Jesus was not there, nor his disciples, they themselves got into the boats and went to Capernaum, seeking Jesus.

²⁵ When they found him on the other side of the sea, they said to him, "Rabbi, when did you come here?" ²⁶ Jesus answered them, "Truly, truly, I say to you, you are seeking me, not because you saw signs, but because you ate your fill of the loaves. ²⁷ Do not work for the food that perishes, but for the food that endures to eternal life, which the Son of Man will give to you. For on him God the Father has set his seal." ²⁸ Then they said to him, "What must we do, to be doing the works of God?" ²⁹ Jesus answered them, "This is the work of God, that you believe in him whom he has sent." ³⁰ So they said to him, "Then what sign do you do, that we may see and believe you? What work do you perform? ³¹ Our fathers ate the manna in the wilderness; as it is written, 'He gave them

bread from heaven to eat.'" [32] Jesus then said to them, "Truly, truly, I say to you, it was not Moses who gave you the bread from heaven, but my Father gives you the true bread from heaven. [33] For the bread of God is he who comes down from heaven and gives life to the world." [34] They said to him, "Sir, give us this bread always."

[35] Jesus said to them, "I am the bread of life; whoever comes to me shall not hunger, and whoever believes in me shall never thirst. [36] But I said to you that you have seen me and yet do not believe. [37] All that the Father gives me will come to me, and whoever comes to me I will never cast out. [38] For I have come down from heaven, not to do my own will but the will of him who sent me. [39] And this is the will of him who sent me, that I should lose nothing of all that he has given me, but raise it up on the last day. [40] For this is the will of my Father, that everyone who looks on the Son and believes in him should have eternal life, and I will raise him up on the last day."

[41] So the Jews grumbled about him, because he said, "I am the bread that came down from heaven." [42] They said, "Is not this Jesus, the son of Joseph, whose father and mother we know? How does he now say, 'I have come down from heaven'?" [43] Jesus answered them, "Do not grumble among yourselves. [44] No one can come to me unless the Father who sent me draws him. And I will raise him up on the last day. [45] It is written in the Prophets, 'And they will all be taught by God.' Everyone who has heard and learned from the Father comes to me— [46] not that anyone has seen the Father except he who is from God; he has seen the Father. [47] Truly, truly, I say to you,

whoever believes has eternal life. ⁴⁸ I am the bread of life. ⁴⁹ Your fathers ate the manna in the wilderness, and they died. ⁵⁰ This is the bread that comes down from heaven, so that one may eat of it and not die. ⁵¹ I am the living bread that came down from heaven. If anyone eats of this bread, he will live forever. And the bread that I will give for the life of the world is my flesh."

⁵² The Jews then disputed among themselves, saying, "How can this man give us his flesh to eat?" ⁵³ So Jesus said to them, "Truly, truly, I say to you, unless you eat the flesh of the Son of Man and drink his blood, you have no life in you. ⁵⁴ Whoever feeds on my flesh and drinks my blood has eternal life, and I will raise him up on the last day. ⁵⁵ For my flesh is true food, and my blood is true drink. ⁵⁶ Whoever feeds on my flesh and drinks my blood abides in me, and I in him. ⁵⁷ As the living Father sent me, and I live because of the Father, so whoever feeds on me, he also will live because of me. ⁵⁸ This is the bread that came down from heaven, not like the bread the fathers ate, and died. Whoever feeds on this bread will live forever." ⁵⁹ Jesus said these things in the synagogue, as he taught at Capernaum.

⁶⁰ When many of his disciples heard it, they said, "This is a hard saying; who can listen to it?" ⁶¹ But Jesus, knowing in himself that his disciples were grumbling about this, said to them, "Do you take offense at this? ⁶² Then what if you were to see the Son of Man ascending to where he was before? ⁶³ It is the Spirit who gives life; the flesh is no help at all. The words that I have spoken to you are spirit and life. ⁶⁴ But there are some of you who do not believe."

(For Jesus knew from the beginning who those were who did not believe, and who it was who would betray him.) [65] And he said, "This is why I told you that no one can come to me unless it is granted him by the Father."

[66] After this many of his disciples turned back and no longer walked with him. [67] So Jesus said to the twelve, "Do you want to go away as well?" [68] Simon Peter answered him, "Lord, to whom shall we go? You have the words of eternal life, [69] and we have believed, and have come to know, that you are the Holy One of God." [70] Jesus answered them, "Did I not choose you, the twelve? And yet one of you is a devil." [71] He spoke of Judas the son of Simon Iscariot, for he, one of the twelve, was going to betray him.

✛ A MODERN STORY ✛

John G. Paton watched as his father turned to walk back home, his long, white hair blowing behind like a victory flag in the wind. James Paton had no doubt his son would overcome and succeed, but John was nervous.

John was headed to Glasgow, about eighty miles from his childhood home in Dumfries, Scotland. He had worked for his father making stockings, but the Lord's call on him was too strong to ignore any longer. John turned north and walked to his new life.

He entered school on a scholarship, pinching pennies and saving money by not eating. His health failed, and he gave up completing school. As he wandered the streets of Glasgow, he thought of returning home, but he knew God wasn't calling him to the stocking factory. Then he saw an advertisement in a window: *Teacher Wanted.*

John began teaching at a small parish school in Glasgow. The students were rough, older men and women who worked all day in the mills. He managed to win their respect and his ministry multiplied.

Over the next ten years John was a missionary to the inner-city poor of Glasgow, but he felt that the Lord was directing him farther from home. Though his friends and congregants pleaded that he stay, John and his young wife, Mary, headed to the New Hebrides islands in the South Seas.

After four months aboard ship the missionaries were grateful to step onto solid ground. It was November 5, 1858. The serene island was covered with thick jungle growth and surrounded by blue water, but the peace was an illusion. John and Mary were greeted on the island of Tanna by naked men trying to attack them. They escaped, only to find out the next day that five native men had been killed and eaten the night before.

The Patons were to bring the message of Jesus to cannibals.

The years that John spent on Tanna were punctuated with constant threats and attacks. But the missionaries only spoke love back to the natives. As time passed, small numbers of the Tannese began to listen. John learned their language and began writing and printing scriptures in their own language. He taught them of the love of God for his children. He offered them gifts of food and clothing.

But not everyone was happy that the Patons were there. Many wished that he would get back on his ship and sail away. Often John was followed by natives swinging clubs, throwing spears, or even pointing muskets. John met the attacks with prayer and by calling aloud on the name of Jehovah. Occasionally a club would hit its mark, but the spears and muskets were unable to harm him. Most often the natives left in fear of the missionaries' God.

The dark jungle hid the natives as well as the white traders who came to the island. The white men often cheated the natives, making the missionaries' work even more difficult. One time a ship arrived with a native who had intentionally been exposed to measles. The man was released to go back to his village and infect the rest of the inhabitants. The tradesman told John that he was doing them a favor.

John and the others ministered to the sick with medicine, food, water, and prayer, but nearly two-thirds of the natives died. They often unwittingly dug their own graves to lie in the cool earth to relieve the fever.

About a year after arriving on Tanna, John's wife gave birth to a son. Shortly after, both died from fever and most likely malaria. John buried them near his hut. The islanders thought he would surely leave now, but they were wrong. John continued reaching out to the natives and was joined by two other missionaries, Mr. and Mrs. Mathieson.

Native children came to the missionaries to learn and find food and comfort. The people of Tanna were still uncivilized, treating family members as competition instead of as loved ones. Women were especially harshly treated. They were considered slaves to serve their husbands. When their husbands died, the wives were strangled so that they could serve their husbands in the hereafter. When enemy tribes fought, they ate the losers in a feast of cannibalistic rejoicing.

John and the Mathiesons stayed about four years on Tanna, but relations with the natives always remained tenuous. The missionaries took turns sleeping so they could watch for danger. Exhaustion finally had its say, and one night all three fell into a deep sleep.

During the night Clutha, John's faithful dog, woke him to warn of danger. John and the Mathiesons arose and began praying in the dark. Soon the room filled with light. The natives were burning the fence around their quarters. John took a revolver and an American tomahawk and told the others to keep praying.

He stepped outside and began chopping the fence down to stop the fire from reaching the house. Half a dozen figures rose from the shadows, yelling, "Kill him! Kill him!" They rushed toward John.

Suddenly a raging tornado came blowing in, sweeping the fire away from the house even as a torrential rain doused the flames. The natives fled in terror, screaming that Jehovah God had rescued his people.

John and the Mathiesons believed it was no longer safe enough to stay on the island. They left the next day for Australia.

John Paton sailed, rode, and walked throughout Australia, Scotland, and England telling the stories of the people in the New Hebrides. Christians offered money and prayers so that John could one day return to the islands.

In 1866, John and his new wife, Margaret, arrived on Aniwa, the closest island to Tanna. Their ministry resembled the mission to Tanna. Cannibalism, fighting, slavery, and all sorts of offenses were common on Aniwa. As before, John started by learning the language.

He managed to make friends with one of the chiefs, Namakei. The chief was interested in what the white man might teach him. Namakei helped John to build a house and several other buildings in the compound. One day John wrote directions on a piece of wood and handed it to Chief Namakei.

"Take this to Mrs. Paton so she can send some supplies," John instructed him.

The chief looked at the wood, thinking it was all a joke. "How will she know what to send?"

"She'll know," John said.

Namakei walked to the house and handed the wood to Mrs. Paton. She read the note and gathered supplies to send back to the work site. Namakei returned, amazed.

"What is this magic wood?" he asked.

John explained written language and read some of the scriptures to Namakei in his own language. He explained that he planned to print the Bible in Namakei's native language. The chief was ecstatic.

When John finished translating, he presented the book to the chief. But instead of happiness, Namakei was distressed that the pages didn't speak to him like they did to John. He needed to learn to read. John took him outside right away and wrote *ABCD* in the dirt. Namakei was a quick learner and soon had the alphabet memorized.

The chief continued learning. Letters became sounds, sounds became words, and words became possibilities. However, when Namakei began reading the printed paper, John realized it was straining the chief's eyes. He needed glasses.

John searched through the supplies sent with him from churches back in Scotland and found a pair of spectacles that would work for Chief Namakei. At first the native thought it was some sort of sorcery, but once convinced that it was safe to wear the glasses, he knew Jesus was real.

"I see it all now! This is what you told us about Jesus. He opened the blind man's eyes. Jesus sent me these glass eyes. I have back my sight!"

It wasn't long until Namakei was asking for "glass eyes" for his wife, who had trouble seeing to sew and cook. She, too, became a believer.

Another problem on Aniwa was not having a source of fresh water. Most people drank from the coconuts and gathered rainwater whenever possible. John decided to dig a well. The natives were certain that he had lost his mind—*Rain only comes from the sky, not the ground.* After digging about thirty feet, they struck water. The natives were quick to give God the credit. None of their gods had ever made rain come from the ground.

As the mission to the New Hebrides expanded, the many missionaries needed a ship to supply their needs. They couldn't depend on traders who cheated and swindled them. A plea was sent out to the supporting churches, and a ship was purchased.

The *Dayspring* was a fine sailing ship that met their needs for several years, but on January 6, 1873, it was caught in a storm and wrecked. Unfortunately the mangled ship was sold by auction to a French slaving company that thought it would be useful in the South Seas. The islanders would recognize the *Dayspring* and rush to it, expecting supplies. They would easily be captured and sold. John and the other missionaries prayed night and day, crying out to God when they discovered the plot.

As the French slavers made their way to the islands, they anchored in a bay and went ashore to celebrate with drinking and feasting. That night as they slept on the shore, a storm blew up and dragged the *Dayspring* along with its anchor onto a reef. The ship's back was irreparably broken in two. The missionaries rejoiced at the answer of a storm. God protected John and the others for many years. Natives intent on killing them often withdrew. Villages that were fighting made peace. Thrown spears were deflected or caught by the intended targets. Tornadoes and hurricanes thwarted the efforts of natives and white men alike.

But the most supernatural story includes the heavenly host.

One night on Aniwa, hostile tribesmen surrounded the compound, drawing close to the house. They intended to burn it down and kill John and his wife. The two of them, locked in the house, prayed on their knees all night. At daybreak John and Margaret were surprised to find themselves alone. The islanders had gone home.

About a year later the chief of that tribe was converted to Christ. John reminded the native of that dark night and asked why the men had abandoned their plot.

The chief explained that they had been frightened when they saw the number of men John and his wife had engaged to defend the missions compound. He said there were hundreds of men in shining garments with drawn swords surrounding the station. The natives had fled in terror.

John knew there were no men engaged for his defense. They were the armies of God defending his territory.

John spent his life reaching out for the hands of the heathen so that he could call them brothers. He finally traveled home on January 28, 1907. Others continued his work on the islands.

In 1980, New Hebrides gained independence and was renamed Vanuatu. Christianity has flourished on the islands.

Nearly 80 percent of islanders claim Christ as their Savior. Cannibalism was long ago given up in favor of the Lord's body.[1]

✥ REFLECTION ✥

Like John the disciple, John Paton was caught in storms. I, too, have been the victim of nature's fury. I have driven on dangerous, snow-covered, icy roads. My wedding was nearly canceled because of a historic blizzard. Creeping across the foggy western ridges of Maryland has caused me great anxiety. Living in Texas taught me to heed tornado sirens. I once watched a twister descend less than a mile from my house. I froze to the spot and prayed.

Hurricanes, blizzards, tsunamis, earthquakes, and wildfires are what make the news. We can try to control the damage they cause, but we can't control them entirely. Forces of nature are beyond our power.

Yet John shows in his gospel that Jesus controls even the winds and waves. John Paton knew that Jesus used nature for his own purposes. And I know to turn to Jesus when his power is the only thing that can save.

1. **Have you ever experienced a supernatural event?**

---

1   This section is based on material from the following sources: Len Garae, "President: Vanuatu has one religion—Christianity," Vanuatu Daily Post, July 10, 2017, accessed July 2018, dailypost.vu/news/president-vanuatu-has-one-religion-christianity/article_1bc334d0-0ff5-50f9-adab-0834da8407dd.html.
John Gibson Paton, The Story of John G. Paton Or Thirty Years Among South Sea Cannibals. (New York: A. L. Burt, 1892).

Sometimes you want to tell a story, but you're afraid of embarrassing someone. Like the time your sister used straight garlic spread on bread because she thought it was a butter spread. The guests tried so hard to eat it, but whew! Or the time your father ran out of gas in Memphis and went the opposite direction of the gas station. The police and a beer bottle were involved.

John was interested in telling the signs of the Messiah, but there were some moments when the apostles didn't look so good, might have even been embarrassed. Walking on the water was one of them. Did you catch that John didn't mention Peter in the scripture reading?

Perhaps he didn't wish to embarrass Peter, though that seems unlikely since he included Peter's denial later in the book. I find it more plausible that he saw Peter's faithlessness as a group attitude. They all had failed Jesus by fearing during the storm and not recognizing him.

I know with all my heart that Jesus is the Christ, the Messiah. But sometimes my faith falters. I hear in my soul, Talk to that stranger, and find myself avoiding their eyes. I know God whispers to give money to an organization, but I think about the taxes that are due this month and put it off. I know God is the Great Physician, but I worry if this lump is more serious than he can handle.

2. **Are you in a storm? Where are your feet—planted in the heaving, rocking boat, or stepping into the foaming sea with Jesus?**

Both are scary, but only one is safe.

In the morning when the masses realized that Jesus was not on the east shore, they got in boats and searched for him. When he was found, Jesus said they weren't looking for him because they had faith in who he was, but because they wanted to be taken care of physically. He then said, "The work of God is this: to believe in the one he has sent" (John 6:29 NIV). That hardly seems like work, until I realize that once I believe, I also feel compelled to action.

I believe that children's faith is important, so I help teach Bible school, chaperone youth trips, and take church kids to dinner. I look forward to times with the youth group, yet I often wish someone else would step up and let me sit on the sidelines.

I believe that everyone needs encouragement, so I write cards or send texts to friends who are struggling. But sometimes I only have good intentions and the cards are never sent.

I believe relationships are part of the church's foundation, so I invite people to lunch, share breakfast with a Christian sister, and host a summer cookout. But more often than not, I go out with the same friends, get takeout and watch Netflix, or schedule a meeting and forget the breakfast.

3. **What do you believe and how are you acting on it? Do you have the attitude of Christ, or do you moan and groan before you *maybe* do it anyway?**
4. **Now do you see why believing in Jesus is hard work?**

Recently my husband and I spit into little vials and sent them off for DNA testing. We found out some interesting things. One of the most interesting is that Matt is descended from the line of King Louis XVI.

Now, it is true that when we dated, I called Matt "Oh Great One," but it was teasing. I had no idea he actually came from royalty. It hasn't changed my behavior toward him, but maybe I should call him "Oh Great One" with a little more respect, or at least a French accent.

Jesus told the crowd in Capernaum that he was better bread than even their ancestors ate when they had the manna that floated down from God in the desert. Knowing Jesus's family and believing that he wasn't anyone special, the Jews began to grumble. They were willing to accept his signs and miracles, but they couldn't get past what they thought they knew about him—he was Joseph's son.

5. **Are you letting something you "know" cloud your vision in seeing the truth?**

✠ ACTION ✠

1. Contemplate your life's storms. Have they resulted in quiet humility, or are you still sinking beneath the waves? End your time of reflection by meditating on Psalm 42. Put your hope in God.

2. What is Jesus asking you to believe, and do you feel compelled to follow through? Are you just following for handouts, or are you offering your hands for the work? Look up today's martyrs on the internet. Read their stories. These are people truly compelled to follow Jesus.

3. Spend time in prayer listening to God. Ask him if there is something you have understood incorrectly

because your human side has made assumptions. Remember, the masses left Jesus after his instruction because it was a hard teaching. Listen carefully, but stay faithful like Peter who said, "We have come to believe and know that you are the Holy One of God" (John 6:69 NIV).

CHAPTER 7

HE NOTICES

✣ A REUNION ✣

"He's just worn out."

Caleb's mother sat down in the kitchen and pulled the little boy onto her shrinking lap. The tears spilling on his cheeks were plugged by a thumb in his mouth. Caleb rested his head against her shoulder.

"Why don't you give him to me?" Sarah lifted her hands out of the dishwater. "I can sing better than I can wash."

The plump old woman felt her way along the wall to the chair in the corner. She sat down with a sigh and then reached her arms toward the sniffling child.

"Come sit with Auntie Sarah." She smiled, still holding out her arms.

"Go on," Caleb's mother said, lifting him off her lap.

Caleb shuffled to Sarah and climbed into her lap. She gathered him up and rested her cheek on his soft hair.

"Now what are these tears all about?" Sarah asked.

"Paul called me a baby," he mumbled, still sucking on his thumb. "He said I can't play with the other boys."

"Mmm. Paul must be your big brother."

Caleb nodded his head against Sarah's bosom and sniffled again.

"I had one of those too. They can be bossy."

"You had a brother?" Caleb looked up at the old woman.

"Yes. He was seventeen years older than I. He was born blind; his eyes couldn't open. Mama and Papa were afraid to have another baby. They didn't want another deformed child."

"Are you blind?"

Sarah smiled. "My eyes don't work so well anymore, but I see inside people just fine. I can see you are a good boy who loves his mother and father very much. I also see that this trip has made you tired and you need some quiet rest."

Caleb pulled his thumb out of his mouth. "Could your brother see inside people like you do?"

The women's laughter in the kitchen danced like dust in a sunbeam.

"Yes, he could," Sarah said. "Would you like to hear a story about him?"

Caleb nestled into the thick arms. Sarah wrapped him more tightly on her lap.

"My brother's name was Saul. He was blind, but he never let that stop him from doing what he wanted. We lived on the edge of Jerusalem. He knew how many steps it took to get to the baker's and the temple. He could tell how straight a piece of wood was just by feeling it. He knew by the smell when it was time to pick the vegetables and harvest the barley."

Sarah rocked side to side and Caleb's eyes began to close.

"But the people in Jerusalem were never satisfied. They wouldn't let Saul do any of those things. Honestly I think they were afraid of him because he looked so different." She paused, her own eyes closed against the memories. "So he had to start begging. Papa was old, and the taxes were very high. There wasn't much he could do to help Saul. We didn't have money like some others."

The women stacked plates on the table while they listened to Sarah's story. A knife sliced through vegetables, making quiet thuds on the cutting board.

"One day when he was sitting there, Jesus walked by, only he didn't know it was Jesus."

Caleb's eyes fluttered open. "How come he didn't know Jesus?"

Sarah's laughter was like rushing water, swooshing over top the little boy's head. "Well, he couldn't see, for one thing." She laughed again. "But mostly I guess because Jesus moved around so much. We'd heard stories, but that was about it."

"I know Jesus," Caleb said. "He looks like my daddy." He snuggled closer and closed his eyes.

"I'm sure he does." The old woman smiled. "There was a crowd of people walking by Saul, not looking at him or anything. There were so many beggars that most people didn't notice them anymore. But Jesus, he stopped.

"He knelt down and talked to my brother. Saul said he could feel Jesus's breath on his face. 'What's your name?' Jesus asked. Nobody ever asked Saul that." Sarah wiped her rheumy eyes. "Then the disciples wanted to know whose fault it was that Saul was blind like that. Jesus told them it wasn't anyone's fault. Then he put some mud on Saul's eyes and told him to go wash in the Pool of Siloam."

Sarah sniffled and then laughed at herself. "I'm just a silly old woman."

"No." Caleb's mother crossed the room and placed her hand on Sarah's shoulder.

Sarah patted her hand and went on with the story. "The pool wasn't far, and Saul went straight on. He said when the mud washed off his face, his eyes opened with it. Just like that." She flashed her fingers and her own glazed eyes grew big. "He was so excited, he started running through the streets, but he realized he didn't know where he was. He traced his way back to the pool and then walked home the way that he had memorized."

Caleb tried to sit up on Sarah's lap. "You mean he wasn't blind?"

"That's right." She nodded and smiled at the little boy.

"Come on; you need a nap." Caleb's mother lifted him off Sarah's knees. "Be right back."

"I'm not tired," Caleb said as he lay his head on his mother's shoulder.

"Fine. You just lie in the other room and listen."

She carried the little boy to the sleeping quarters and set him on the pallet. He was asleep before she could pull up the coverlet.

Sarah's voice continued to drift through the house: "Mama and Papa were overwhelmed. I was twelve by then, big enough to know what was going on. You'd think people would've been happy for Saul, but instead it became a big problem."

The dishes were done, and the pot of stew simmered over the grate. The women gathered around Sarah, some on the floor, a few on the bench. Caleb's mother lowered herself to the bench.

"Saul rushed in the house and scared me. I thought he was some demon-possessed man the way he was going on. I recognized Saul's voice, and I guess I could tell it was him, but his face was different now. I just stood there staring at him, my mouth hanging open. He probably thought I was an imbecile." She chuckled.

"What did your parents say?" one of the younger women asked.

"Mama was in the garden and she came in when she heard all the yelling. She sat down on the bed and just cried and cried. Papa wasn't home then; I remember that. The neighbors came in to see what was going on. Some wouldn't believe Saul, and Mama was crying so much that they thought she had lost her mind."

"No wonder," the young woman murmured.

"I suppose they meant to be kind, but it turned into a mob really quick. Some men grabbed hold of Saul and took him off to the council. Thought they'd get to the bottom of it and lock him up, I guess. I just remember Mama crying and screaming as they dragged Saul away. The baker's wife held Mama down in the house."

Sarah took a deep breath and exhaled slowly. Her chest shuddered as the memory was released. "Saul tried telling everyone that, yes, it was him and what had happened. The Pharisees, though, were intent on stopping all the talk about Jesus. They accused Saul of making up the story to incite the people. Like he was a criminal!"

The old woman's blind eyes flashed holy fire. "They wouldn't believe Saul until they sent for Mama and Papa. I wasn't allowed to go, but I know they were scared. Everyone knew if you supported Jesus, you were shunned. Not allowed to attend the synagogue. Not part of the community. Life was already so hard.

"So, Papa, well … I guess he did what he felt he had to do. He said that Saul was his blind son, but he would have to speak for himself since he was a grown man. Papa reasoned we could still help Saul on occasion if he was thrown out.

"But Saul didn't put up with their foolishness. He told the Pharisees and anyone who would listen that it was Jesus who had healed him. It went on for days. They were cruel, accusing Saul of some sort of conspiracy, then saying he was a sinner and deserved to be blind, then turning it all on Jesus. I don't know how Saul stood it."

"He was strong, like you," Caleb's mother said. "He knew the truth, and he was free."

Her voice caressed the old woman, and she smiled.

"Free. Yes, that's it. He was free." Sarah nodded her head. "He chose Jesus and ended up leading several of those hateful men to the Messiah. I guess my blind brother opened more than his own eyes." She exhaled.

"That's right." The younger women agreed.

Sarah stood up, catching herself on the chair back when her knees tried to buckle. "Now I think I'll go take a nap with that little one. I'm worn out too."

✢ An Ancient Story ✢
(John 9 – 10:21)

Chapter 9 of John begins with the disciples asking Jesus a question. We would find it insensitive today, but they had a legitimate question for the time they lived in: *Did this man sin, or was it his parents' sin that caused his blindness?* The Pharisees and scribes had been debating that for years.

It may seem odd to us, because we don't blame sin for children's disabilities, but we do still face the question for ourselves. Often I have heard people say they must have done something wrong for God to be punishing them. They equate their suffering with a punishment from God.

Jesus said that wasn't it at all. This man's blindness was an opportunity to show God's glory. But, he warned, the time was short. Night was coming.

1. **Remember John's "light" references? What do you suppose John meant by inserting a "night" reference here?**

How did Jesus heal the man? He spit on the ground and made mud. Jesus must have had some active salivary glands! Mud made with spittle would take quite awhile to produce.

Imagine the disciples, the crowds, the waiting blind man. What were they thinking? What were they expecting?

2. **Do you watch Jesus in wonder? Do you still have a sense of his miraculous abilities?**

The blind man must have been so confused at his inquisition. Sight was a new thing for him. He was excited, ecstatic. He wanted to tell people the wonderful thing that had happened to him, but instead he was put on trial.

The people who should have loved him the most were afraid to help him. His own parents threw him under the horse cart and said he should answer for himself. I'd like to give them the benefit of the doubt and think that they were planning to help him after things cooled down, but the now-seeing man would not have known that.

So there he was—stunned, on trial, forsaken by his parents—and he defended Jesus. He had been healed and he knew who the healer was.

3. **What about you? Do you stand strong and defend Jesus?**

The healing practices of other religions in ancient civilizations often included mud. Asclepius was one such healer god. Often followers of Asclepius were prescribed mud-and-water treatments for their illnesses. Though the Jews of Jesus's time were not significantly monotheistic, it would be possible to condemn Jesus for practicing magical arts or calling on the name of another god.

As you read, notice in verse 24 that the Jews brought the blind man back again. They wanted him to be completely honest, saying, "Give glory to God." It would be similar to today's version of "tell the truth, the whole truth, and nothing but the truth, so help you God." And then they asked again for the impetus of the healing. They seemed to be searching for a way to trap Jesus—nothing new there.

They weren't hard of hearing. They weren't daft. They were lawyers looking for the loophole, the fine print, the missing link.

4. **In what ways do you try to "trap" Jesus?**

Verses 30-33 are reminiscent of Jesus's dark encounter with Nicodemus in chapter 3 of John. The blind man expected that those charged with teaching the people about God ought to have been able to recognize God's work when they saw it.

The Israelites knew of prophets with amazing abilities. Elijah stopped the rain for over three years. Then he made it rain after a spiritual battle ending with fire and lightning from heaven (1 Kings 17-18). Elisha raised the dead and fed the hungry (2 Kings 4). Daniel was saved in the lions' den (Daniel 6). Samson had supernatural strength (Judges 13-16). Gideon found fleeces in varying degrees of dampness (Judges 6).

Yet here was Jesus showing all those signs and more, but the Pharisees couldn't see that he was from God.

Then John spends the first part of chapter 10 showing that the Pharisees were the blind ones because they couldn't hear!

Do you hear the shepherd's voice? Do you know who to follow? Does your instinct shout one thing when your sight—or blindness—tells you another?

5. **Are you, like the healed blind man, strong in your defense of Jesus, or are you, like the Jews of verse 19, divided?**

JOHN 9

[1] As he passed by, he saw a man blind from birth. [2] And his disciples asked him, "Rabbi, who sinned, this man or his parents, that he was born blind?" [3] Jesus answered, "It was not that this man sinned, or his parents, but that the works of God might be displayed in him. [4] We must work the works of him who sent me while it is day; night is coming, when no one can work. [5] As long as I am in the world, I am the light of the world." [6] Having said these things, he spit on the ground and made mud with the saliva. Then he anointed the man's eyes with the mud [7] and said to him, "Go, wash in the pool of Siloam" (which means Sent). So he went and washed and came back seeing.

⁸ The neighbors and those who had seen him before as a beggar were saying, "Is this not the man who used to sit and beg?" ⁹ Some said, "It is he." Others said, "No, but he is like him." He kept saying, "I am the man." ¹⁰ So they said to him, "Then how were your eyes opened?" ¹¹ He answered, "The man called Jesus made mud and anointed my eyes and said to me, 'Go to Siloam and wash.' So I went and washed and received my sight." ¹² They said to him, "Where is he?" He said, "I do not know."

¹³ They brought to the Pharisees the man who had formerly been blind. ¹⁴ Now it was a Sabbath day when Jesus made the mud and opened his eyes. ¹⁵ So the Pharisees again asked him how he had received his sight. And he said to them, "He put mud on my eyes, and I washed, and I see." ¹⁶ Some of the Pharisees said, "This man is not from God, for he does not keep the Sabbath." But others said, "How can a man who is a sinner do such signs?" And there was a division among them. ¹⁷ So they said again to the blind man, "What do you say about him, since he has opened your eyes?" He said, "He is a prophet."

¹⁸ The Jews did not believe that he had been blind and had received his sight, until they called the parents of the man who had received his sight ¹⁹ and asked them, "Is this your son, who you say was born blind? How then does he now see?" ²⁰ His parents answered, "We know that this is our son and that he was born blind. ²¹ But how he now sees we do not know, nor do we know who opened his eyes. Ask him; he is of age. He will speak for himself." ²² (His parents said these things because they

feared the Jews, for the Jews had already agreed that if anyone should confess Jesus to be Christ, he was to be put out of the synagogue.) [23] Therefore his parents said, "He is of age; ask him."

[24] So for the second time they called the man who had been blind and said to him, "Give glory to God. We know that this man is a sinner." [25] He answered, "Whether he is a sinner I do not know. One thing I do know, that though I was blind, now I see." [26] They said to him, "What did he do to you? How did he open your eyes?" [27] He answered them, "I have told you already, and you would not listen. Why do you want to hear it again? Do you also want to become his disciples?" [28] And they reviled him, saying, "You are his disciple, but we are disciples of Moses. [29] We know that God has spoken to Moses, but as for this man, we do not know where he comes from." [30] The man answered, "Why, this is an amazing thing! You do not know where he comes from, and yet he opened my eyes. [31] We know that God does not listen to sinners, but if anyone is a worshiper of God and does his will, God listens to him. [32] Never since the world began has it been heard that anyone opened the eyes of a man born blind. [33] If this man were not from God, he could do nothing." [34] They answered him, "You were born in utter sin, and would you teach us?" And they cast him out.

[35] Jesus heard that they had cast him out, and having found him he said, "Do you believe in the Son of Man?" [36] He answered, "And who is he, sir, that I may believe in him?" [37] Jesus said to him, "You have seen him, and it is he who is speaking to you." [38] He said, "Lord, I believe,"

and he worshiped him. ³⁹ Jesus said, "For judgment
I came into this world, that those who do not see may
see, and those who see may become blind." ⁴⁰ Some of the
Pharisees near him heard these things, and said to him,
"Are we also blind?" ⁴¹ Jesus said to them, "If you were
blind, you would have no guilt; but now that you say, 'We
see,' your guilt remains.

———

JOHN 10:1-21

¹ "Truly, truly, I say to you, he who does not enter the
sheepfold by the door but climbs in by another way,
that man is a thief and a robber. ² But he who enters
by the door is the shepherd of the sheep. ³ To him the
gatekeeper opens. The sheep hear his voice, and he calls
his own sheep by name and leads them out. ⁴ When he
has brought out all his own, he goes before them, and the
sheep follow him, for they know his voice. ⁵ A stranger
they will not follow, but they will flee from him, for they
do not know the voice of strangers." ⁶ This figure of speech
Jesus used with them, but they did not understand what
he was saying to them.

⁷ So Jesus again said to them, "Truly, truly, I say to you,
I am the door of the sheep. ⁸ All who came before me
are thieves and robbers, but the sheep did not listen to
them. ⁹ I am the door. If anyone enters by me, he will be
saved and will go in and out and find pasture. ¹⁰ The thief
comes only to steal and kill and destroy. I came that they
may have life and have it abundantly. ¹¹ I am the good

shepherd. The good shepherd lays down his life for the sheep. [12] He who is a hired hand and not a shepherd, who does not own the sheep, sees the wolf coming and leaves the sheep and flees, and the wolf snatches them and scatters them. [13] He flees because he is a hired hand and cares nothing for the sheep. [14] I am the good shepherd. I know my own and my own know me, [15] just as the Father knows me and I know the Father; and I lay down my life for the sheep. [16] And I have other sheep that are not of this fold. I must bring them also, and they will listen to my voice. So there will be one flock, one shepherd. [17] For this reason the Father loves me, because I lay down my life that I may take it up again. [18] No one takes it from me, but I lay it down of my own accord. I have authority to lay it down, and I have authority to take it up again. This charge I have received from my Father."

[19] There was again a division among the Jews because of these words. [20] Many of them said, "He has a demon, and is insane; why listen to him?" [21] Others said, "These are not the words of one who is oppressed by a demon. Can a demon open the eyes of the blind?"

✢ A MODERN STORY ✢

1967. America reeked of fear. Its acrid smoke burned from Michigan to Florida. On college campuses the smell of fear turned young people's hope to charcoal ashes. The nightly news puffed dark billows from sea to troubled sea. Even sleepy Mid-west towns raised their faces to the wind and turned in fear.

America was firmly entrenched in Vietnam. Race riots spread across the United States, while the Great Race to the moon stalled when Apollo 1 went up in flames on the launching pad, killing three astronauts.

Young men feared being killed in action. White people feared black people. And everyone feared Russia gaining ground and annihilating America with nuclear warheads.

But George Baker didn't smell fear. He played ball with his young son and sneezed the summer dust that filled his nose. He breathed deeply of long leaf pine while hunting in the fall. He attended church pot lucks in winter and caught whiffs of smoked pork and warm cornbread. And when winter was over, he exhaled and started again with the fresh smells of spring.

His life was filled with the good scents of home in Tarboro, North Carolina.

George Baker worked hard, took care of his family, and trusted God. He had no time for fear. His wife, Pat, took care of the children, kept a tidy home, and loved George with all her heart. It was a good life. A simple life.

"Hurry up, George. You're going to be late. The children are already at school." Pat stood at the door, lunchbox in hand. "The men will never believe you were hunting all this time and didn't get a thing."

George pulled his jacket on one arm, kissed his wife, and grabbed the metal box she offered. He flipped the jacket up and kept on running out of the house, catching his arm on the door frame.

"I'll get a big one tomorrow," he called over his shoulder.

Pat waved from the glass storm door until George backed out of the drive. Leaves littered the front yard and she sighed. The afternoon's work was piling up on the front lawn.

———

George slipped through the metal door and hung up his jacket. He clocked in and headed to his spot on the assembly line. Anaconda made telephone cables, and George wound them onto the bobbins.

Men lifted hands in greeting as George passed; their smirks told him that Mr. Calvin was waiting down the line for him.

"Hey, Mr. Calvin," George said as he positioned himself in front of the machines. "Sorry I'm late. A big buck got away from me."

"I know some other big bucks that are getting away from you." Calvin shook his head and made a mark on his clipboard. "You'll be docked for being late."

"Yes, sir." George nodded and flipped on the winder.

———

The morning passed winding phone cables on large wooden bobbins. The full bobbins were shipped down the line and loaded into the dock area. Trucks passed in and out of the factory, the smell of diesel mixing with the hot metallic odor of the cables.

But George could still smell the morning's damp earth. Fog had drifted across the field obstructing his view. He would get that buck tomorrow.

The bobbin was full. George hit the stop button, but something caught and crimped the heavy spool. The pin sheared off as the jog button jammed. Without thinking, George stuck his arm into the mass of cables to save it from further damage.

The clutch hung up and caught his arm in the swirl of metal. His forearm broke in half and the front was pushed out the end of the elbow.

"Hit the stop button!" he yelled to the safety supervisor.

Machinery ground to a halt. Men came running from all areas of the factory. Blood poured out from the round of cables and spilled on the concrete floor.

"Help me out here," George called to the men.

One of the workers helped George pull his arm loose. Now the blood flowed freely. Several men went weak in the knees, but George was high on adrenaline.

"Lie down," his supervisor said as he tried to force George to the floor. "You're going to faint."

"I ain't going to faint. Bring me a bandage to wrap around this. I need to get to the ER." George held his right arm together with his left hand. "Come on now. Get the first aid kit and help me out."

"I'll get it George," one of the men called and took off for the office.

"Here. Wrap this copper wire around your arm. You're going to bleed out." Another guy down the line came at him with some thin wire.

"Didn't you listen in that class last week? We just went over this." George shook his head and turned away from the wire. "I'll lose my arm if I do that. Just get me a bandage. I'll drive myself over to the hospital."

"Don't be foolish." Mr. Calvin was there now. "The ambulance is on the way."

George could hear the siren getting closer.

———

"Hey, bud. What happened to you?" Dr. Robinson grinned as he came around the curtained triage. He lifted the stethoscope to his ears and listened to George's strong heartbeat. "You're doing alright, but we have to wait for your wife to sign the papers."

"Don't you call Pat. She'll be a mess." George tried to sit up, but a nurse pushed him back down. "I can sign any papers you have. I'm left-handed."

"Are you sure you're up to it?" The doctor furrowed his brow.

"Of course, I am. You just put my arm together so God can heal it."

George signed the paper and lay back against the bed. The choking smell of anesthetic filled his nose and throat.

———

When George woke up his arm was encased in a plaster cast. The surgeon was hopeful that he would be able to use the arm and hand again in a few months. The fingers were sewn back in place and the arm bones were manipulated back to their original positions.

"I look like little George, Jr." George smiled at his wife sitting in the chair by the bed. "I'll have to get him to sign my cast like all his buddies signed his."

"Yours is a might more complicated than Junior's." Pat smiled, but tears filled her blue eyes. "Thank God you're alright."

———

After a week or two, Mr. Calvin called George.

"You think you can come back to work yet and do a few things?"

"Course I can." George laughed. "It'd take more than a broken arm to keep me down."

"Well you just do what you can and don't mess that arm up anymore," Mr. Calvin said. "Like I said, just do what you can and if anyone bothers you, you send them down to me."

George straightened things up at the factory, mostly piddling around since the cast was always in the way. The men were friendly and encouraging. Even George's supervisor was happy to see him.

Winter deepened and George followed doctor's orders as much as he could stand. He wanted to do more, but everyone else was anxious to help him.

"How's it look, doc?"

George sat up on the bed and rolled his sleeve over the cast.

"Well, George." Doctor Robinson hesitated. "It looks like you're going to need another surgery."

George shook his head and wiggled his fingers.

"No," he said. "I can move my hand just fine. Lookey there."

He wiggled the fingers again. The flesh was still a bit swollen, but the hand was working as it should.

"Not your hand, George. It's the bone. It isn't healing like it should." Doctor Robinson held up the X-ray. "You need a piece of your hip bone taken out and put into the arm."

Pat drew in a deep breath. George looked over at her and grinned. He patted her hand and turned back to the doctor.

"I can't do it," the doctor explained, "but over in Little Washington there's a guy that's had some success. If anyone can fix you up again, it's him."

"Well, if you think I ought to go see him, I will. But I already told you, it ain't a doctor that'll fix my arm. God told me he'd heal it."

———

A few weeks later, George entered the hospital in Washington, North Carolina. Dr. Swain explained the procedure to George and sent him over to X-ray to take some more pictures of the fracture.

George settled for the night in the hospital bed, but he didn't feel right about the surgery. The night wore on and George tossed and turned in bed. Finally, at sunrise, he wandered to the end of the hallway and stared at the pink and yellow sky through the window.

"Lord, I believe you said you were going to heal this here arm. Now if you want me to have surgery, I will, but I don't think that's what you meant."

He squinted in the sun's glare. A great peace filled him and the dull ache of the arm disappeared.

"What are you doing out here?" A nurse scolded him. "You should be asleep by now. That sedative is going to kick in any minute."

"I need to see Dr. Swain." George looked at the nurse. "I need an X-ray."

The nurse shuffled George back to the room. Dr. Swain turned the corner.

"What are you doing up, George?"

"I want you to take a picture of my arm. I don't think I need surgery."

"George, we already took fifteen pictures of that arm, five yesterday. You need surgery." Dr. Swain placed his hand on

George's arm. "You're going to be alright. I've done this surgery before."

"But you don't need to; that's what I'm telling you." George stood up taller. "I think God healed me. Just take another picture. I'll pay for it myself."

Dr. Swain agreed to let George have one more X-ray and then they administered the anesthetic. George sank into a deep sleep.

———

George woke to the smell of hospital food. His stomach lurched.

"You're awake." Pat smiled at him and stroked his cheek.

"What did they decide?" George asked.

"There wasn't anything to decide." Pat smiled ear-to-ear. "Your arm is whole."

Dr. Swain walked in swinging his clipboard. He picked up his stethoscope and listened to George's heart.

"Seems you know a bit more about doctoring than you let on." Dr. Swain smiled and put the stethoscope around his neck. "Your arm is going to be fine. The bone has joined together just like you said."

"I told you God was going to heal it." George took a deep breath and grinned. "But don't you worry, doc. I'll make sure you come out smelling like a rose."[1]

———

1   This section is based on material from the following source: George and Pat Baker, interview by Traci L. Stead, June 15, 2019.

✠ Reflection ✠

True-life, modern stories of healing are hard to prove unless you yourself have experienced them. You can easily find stories on Christian television or radio. There are accounts on blogs, professional websites, and in magazines. Some accounts are from famous people, celebrities who give credit to Christ for their healing. When you don't know the person, the situation, or the complete story, it's easy to doubt.

1. **Do you believe in modern miracles of healing? If so, have you witnessed any?**

I can tell you about my older son's leg that was shorter than the other by a couple of inches, and after prayer by the church it grew and was equal to the opposite leg. I can tell you about a family friend who had Reye's syndrome and her life hung in the balance, but after spiritual intervention she was healed. One of my dearest friends had cancer, and though the treatment included radiation therapy, she believes that it was God who allowed the radiation to heal her. Most recently a rattlesnake bit our youngest son. An online call went out via social media, and prayers commenced around the world. By the power of God, and the strong antivenin, he was spared a horrible experience and healed quickly and completely.

2. **Do you count a healing as a gift from God if doctors and medicine were involved? Why or why not?**
3. **Can you justify your answer with any scriptures?**

In 2017, I was attending a church service in another state. A special prayer request was made during Bible class for a member of that congregation. A woman struggling with an advanced form of cancer was now in grave danger. Two separate infections were racing through her body.

The woman was already in a special unit at the hospital that was supposed to be extra-sterile. Because of the new attack the CDC was called in. The prognosis was dire: *She won't survive.*

But this little church didn't believe that the CDC held any power. They didn't succumb to the fear and negativity that threatened despair. Instead they prayed.

They prayed in Bible class. They prayed in the worship assembly. I accompanied some to the hospital to pray outside her unit. An online twenty-four-hour prayer vigil was devised, and her case was taken to the Father in uninterrupted pleading. They begged for this woman's health to be returned to her.

Three days later the CDC, the hospital, the doctors, and nurses were all proved wrong when she went home healed from the infections. It was a miracle of healing.

4. Have you ever been part of a group prayer for healing? What was the outcome?

Some will question whether this was a miracle. *Miracles* in our vocabulary mean something supernatural and, dare we say it, unbelievable. But for John, and it would seem for Jesus, a miracle was a sign. But why does God not heal everyone? Why do so many prayers for healing go unanswered?

I'm not sure. But what I do know is that sometimes God wants to show us something.

The woman that others and I prayed over was healed of that problem, but she was not healed of the cancer—not yet, anyway.

Perhaps the healing was a sign that God is listening. Perhaps it was a blessing from the Father to his children who had faith that he can still heal.

———

The United States government has spent millions of dollars researching whether intercessory prayer is effective in healing. Many studies later the research is inconclusive. One study followed a thousand heart patients after surgery. The patients were secretly divided into two groups: one group was prayed for while the other was not. Neither group knew prayer was a factor in their medical regimen.

All the patients were followed for a year, and then a third party was asked to look at their files using a preset group of criteria to see how they were faring. The third party did not know which patients were prayed over and which were not. The patients who were prayed for had 11 percent fewer heart attacks, strokes, and life-threatening complications.

No one in the medical field can say for certain that prayer helps or doesn't help a patient; they aren't willing to discontinue medicine or other therapies in favor of prayer-only prescriptions. But for those physicians who believe in the power of prayer, there is benefit in adding prayer to the doctor appointments and visits.

I firmly believe this woman experienced a miraculous healing, but I have also witnessed prayer that fails to result in physical healing. I don't believe this is a lack of faith on the part of the patient or the person(s) praying. Jesus did not heal everyone he met. That was not his mission.

His mission was to lead people back to the Father through teaching and signs. His mission continues to this day.[2]

5. **How do you use sickness, disability, or disease to point others to Jesus?**

The blind man in John was miraculously healed. But many other blind men were not. The blindness and its struggles were not the mission of Christ. Pointing to the Father was.

George and Pat Baker's son, Michael, died from leukemia when he was sixteen. I asked the Bakers why George was healed and Michael wasn't. Pat answered, "I don't know why. But I know there is healing, and then there is Ultimate Healing. Michael received the best healing."

The Bakers live to point others to Jesus and the Father. That's the best sign you'll ever see.

---

2   This section includes information based on material from the following sources:

"Can Prayer Heal?" ABC News, Aug. 10, 2001, accessed August 2017, abcnews.go.com/2020/story?id=132674&page=1.

Larry Dossey, Healing Words: The Power of Prayer and The Practice of Medicine (San Francisco: Harper San Francisco, 1993).

Gerald Saliman, "The Prayer Prescription," The Permanente Journal, National Center for Biotechnology Information, Spring 2010, accessed August 2017, ncbi.nlm.nih.gov/pmc/articles/PMC2912708/.

"Science Proves the Healing Power of Prayer," Newsmax, March 31, 2015, accessed August 2017, newsmax.com/Health/Headline/prayer-health-faith-medicine/2015/03/31/id/635623/.

✛ ACTION ✛

1. There are consequences to sin. Consequences are not the same as punishment. Jesus has already suffered the punishment for your sins. All of them. Are you struggling with guilt? Do you feel like God is punishing you for some egregious sin? Spend this week reading Romans chapter 8. Read it daily. Read it in several versions. Memorize the parts you struggle to believe. Allow the Spirit to speak for you in your pain.

2. There are occasions when God will heal. Many believers and nonbelievers alike say prayer and healings are just coincidences. All I know is that when I pray, "coincidences" sometimes happen. When I don't pray, there are none. Is there someone you need to be praying for? Take this time to ask God for a miracle that will point to him. Be prepared to accept whatever that miracle may look like. Remember, the miracle of salvation looked like the death of the Father's only Son.

3. Some people must struggle through life without healing. The blind man was sent out to beg. He was ostracized and isolated. The Bakers experienced great loss and future suffering. It is no cliché that we are to be the healing hands of Jesus. You can bear someone's burden with them and lighten the load. Visit the NICU and hold the dying babies. Serve at the homeless shelter and sit at the table with the

people. Keep the single mom's children for a week so she can visit her mother. Donate blood. Buy some groceries. Sit on the park bench and visit with the parents of special needs kids. Notice the people you pass. Do this so that "the works of God might be displayed" (John 9:3).

CHAPTER 8

HE DELIVERS

✢ A REUNION ✢

Sparks flew toward the sky like summer's abundant fireflies. The evening air was damp and chilly. The autumn leaves would soon light their own fire across the land.

"Will there be a story tonight?"

Caleb licked the sweet honey from his fingers and looked at his mother. She sat on the ground next to him, rubbing her swollen belly.

"Yes. A very special story. John will tell this one."

"Will it be a scary story again?" Caleb's eyes were wide. "I don't like scary stories."

"You're a big baby. I'm not afraid of some ghost story," Paul said.

"I am not a baby!"

"Boys," their mother said, raising her eyebrows. "The beds are waiting."

They hung their heads, afraid to look at their mother. To go to bed early was a fate worse than sitting with the girls.

"Feeling alright?" Caleb's father sat down with them, looking at his wife.

"Yes, just tired." She smiled and sighed.

"Is everyone ready for a story?" The old man walked into the circle of light.

The children cheered, and several birds flew out of the tree above. Their black silhouettes raced across the darkening sky.

"This story is about one of Jesus's friends. His name was Lazarus, and he had two sisters, Mary and Martha."

"I'm glad we don't have any sisters," Caleb said as he leaned against his mother's arm.

"Be careful what you say. This might be a little girl and she just heard you."

Caleb stared at his mother's middle, then turned back to John.

"We often visited Lazarus and his sisters when we walked from Galilee to Jerusalem. They lived in Bethany, just outside Jerusalem. Lazarus was blessed. Mary and Martha were good cooks. They made the best honey-soaked figs."

"See? A sister could be a good thing," Caleb's mother whispered and patted her bulging middle.

Caleb tilted his head and eyed his mother's tummy. "Do you think she knows how to make raisin cakes?"

She laughed and pulled him close.

"We were staying across the Jordan, back where John used to baptize in the early days, when a message came from Judea. Lazarus was sick, and his sisters were worried. We thought maybe Jesus would tell the messenger to go home, that Lazarus was healed, but instead he just got quiet.

"People were always hanging around, and we didn't have time to think about it. Someone else came and asked for his healing touch and that was the end of it as far as I knew." John shrugged his shoulders.

"Did Lazarus get better?" Caleb asked as he sat up on his knees.

"No." John shook his head and looked around the group. "It was two days later when Jesus told us he was heading back to Judea. The crowds were big where we were, and the last time we were in Judea, they had tried to stone Jesus. It just didn't make any sense. You don't sneak into a lion's den when your own house has plenty."

Waves lapped at the shore and a fisherman's call rang out over the water. Fog drifted at the edge of the firelight.

"We tried to stop him from going, but he was intent. 'Lazarus has died. We need to go to him.'" John laughed. "That made as much sense as putting a worm on a hook after the fish is in your bucket."

Everyone laughed along with him.

"Thomas was ready to defend Jesus, though. He convinced us all to go too. When we got close to Bethany, we met mourners headed that way from Jerusalem. They said Lazarus had already been in the grave for four days.

"The crowd was clamoring for Jesus. He never got a break. It was tiresome." John sighed and paused. "Then Martha came rushing up to Jesus. She was crying and angry. She wanted to know why he hadn't come before it was too late for Lazarus.

"Jesus told her Lazarus would rise again, but she wanted more than the resurrection. She wanted her brother. Instead Jesus asked to see her sister."

John sat down on an upturned stump. He put his hands on his knees and stared at the ground. The crackling fire mixed with the lapping of the waves. Everyone was quiet.

John looked up. His cheeks were wet. "My brother James always made fun of me for crying so easily. I couldn't stand to see an animal in pain. I once cried over a donkey that had to be killed after it broke its leg in a hole. He used to call me a big baby."

Paul looked at Caleb and poked him with a finger.

"But that day Jesus was the one crying. He took Mary and Martha in his arms and cried with them, just like Lazarus was his own brother."

Caleb scrunched his face at Paul and stuck out his tongue.

"People were whispering accusations. 'Couldn't he have helped Lazarus? He healed so many, why not his own friend? He opened the eyes of the blind; this would've been easy.' I know how they felt. Jesus befuddled me many times."

John breathed in deep through his nose and then blew all his air out. He stood, stretched, and walked toward the fire.

"Jesus wanted to see the tomb where they laid Lazarus, so we all went together. It was a big cave with a stone in front of it." John circled his arms above the fire to show the size. "Jesus wanted them to remove the stone. Martha protested. Lazarus had been dead four days."

John turned to look at everyone. The corners of his mouth lifted. "She thought he didn't understand. The truth was, we didn't understand."

A few people chuckled, while others murmured agreement.

"Finally Martha agreed to open the tomb. I helped roll away the stone. Then Jesus just stood there, talking like he would do when he was praying. He said he was praying for our benefit and then he faced the tomb. We waited, but nothing happened. I remember Martha biting her nails and Mary looked like she was going to faint." John turned back to the fire and lifted his arms. "Then Jesus said, 'Come out, Lazarus.'"

A man jumped through the fire and landed in front of Paul. The boy yelped and jumped in his father's lap.

"Big baby!" Caleb laughed and rolled on the ground.

John and all the others laughed.

"That's about how I reacted," John said and reached down to pat Paul's head. "It's frightening to see a dead man walk out of a tomb."

Paul tried to laugh, but tears stung his eyes. His father held him close and kissed his head.

"The next tomb I saw couldn't keep hold of its victim either. When Jesus rose from the dead, it was the final sign. He was … and is … the Messiah."

✦ AN ANCIENT STORY ✦
(JOHN 11 – 12:11)

In chapter 11, John tells us that Jesus loved Mary, Martha, and Lazarus, and after learning Lazarus was sick, Jesus "stayed where he was two more days" (v. 6 NIV). That just doesn't scream love, now does it? But Jesus had a plan that only he knew.

The time frame seems to suggest that Lazarus might have died while the messenger traveled to Jesus. Jesus waited two days and then went to the sisters. Whatever the timing of the message and the death, we know that Lazarus had been dead at least four days when Jesus arrived.

Common Jewish belief was that the body had a chance of resurrection up to three days after death. After the third day the spirit would be completely separated from the body and couldn't return. Jesus allowed Lazarus to be dead for four days.

This final sign was intended to prove without a doubt that he was—and is—the Christ, the Messiah.

1. **What other scriptures show people being raised from the dead?**

2. **How is this incident different from the others?**

Sometimes I walk in the early evening. I remember one autumn walking the dog through the fields at dusk. The darkness fell more quickly than I had expected, and I hadn't brought a flashlight with me. Coyotes howled at the edge of the tree line. I picked up my pace and headed home.

In verse 8, the disciples were concerned about going back to Jerusalem and Judea, but Jesus told them that while they had the light, it would be alright.

Later, in 12:35-36 (NIV), he said, "You are going to have the light just a little while longer. Walk while you have the light, before darkness overtakes you. Whoever walks in the dark does not know where they are going. Believe in the light while you have the light, so that you may become children of light."

3. **Do you know where you are going? What are you using for light?**

In 11:4, Jesus said that Lazarus's sickness would not end in death. Perhaps that explains why they didn't understand the sleep euphemism in 11:11. In verse 14, he plainly told them that Lazarus had died.

Yet they didn't seem to get that Jesus was going to bring Lazarus back to life. Instead they focused on the atmosphere in Jerusalem. They expected a fight and likely death.

We might say they couldn't see the forest for the trees.

Jesus had great things planned, but the disciples were worried about other problems. *If Lazarus is dead, then it's just time to move on. Why put yourself, and us, in danger?* they wondered.

4. **What is your focus? Are you perhaps missing the forest for the trees?**

Martha was the first sister to meet with Jesus. She and he had a long conversation about resurrection, in which it seemed that she understood that Lazarus would be resurrected. She believed in the resurrection, and she believed that Jesus was the Messiah and the Son of God.

But when they arrived at the tomb, it was Martha who tried to stop Jesus from opening the tomb. "It's too late," she basically said.

Her mouth professed belief in Jesus, but her body told another story.

I have a friend who prays, but she doesn't expect answers. Another friend believes God will care for him, but he squirrels away money like it all rests on his own shoulders. And another friend says she believes in Jesus's grace and mercy, but she isn't convinced that she has his favor.

5. **In what ways do you say, "Yes, Lord I believe ..." but your behavior says something different?**

Jesus told the disciples that the situation was not what it appeared to be, that God would be glorified. He told Martha that her brother would be resurrected. Mary and the mourners fell at his feet, weeping in hopelessness.

The NIV and other modern translations tell us that this scene caused Jesus to weep and to be greatly troubled. We get the feeling that he had a special relationship with the family of siblings and that he was truly saddened at the death of a friend.

However, that is misleading. When John says Jesus was "deeply moved," he means he was perturbed, irritated. It was considered a stern warning. He asked to be led to the tomb, and again he was troubled; we might say angered.

He was the answer to life in death. He was the solution to their sadness, but they couldn't see it.

This was the same emotion Jesus expressed in Matthew 23 and Luke 13, when he mourned Jerusalem's refusal of him. It was the same frustration he felt when his disciples were unable to support him in the garden.

So, in verse 39 when Jesus told them to move the stone, he was irritated that Martha wanted to argue the point. He went on to say, "Did I not tell you…?"

Have you ever felt that? You know the answer, you explain the answer, and no one believes you. Multiply that feeling by about three years and you get what Jesus is going through.

6. **How do you react to Jesus when he says, "Trust me," but everything looks impossibly ridiculous?**

John used the resurrection of Lazarus as the final scene of Jesus's signs of the Messiahship. It seemed to have been an effective sign, because John tells us the people believed in him. They also went to Jerusalem to tell the Pharisees.

Most likely they expected the Pharisees would welcome Jesus to the table—and expected that the Pharisees would be thrilled to find the Christ after all those years of waiting.

How wrong they were.

JOHN 11

¹ Now a certain man was ill, Lazarus of Bethany, the village of Mary and her sister Martha. ² It was Mary who anointed the Lord with ointment and wiped his feet with her hair, whose brother Lazarus was ill. ³ So the sisters sent to him, saying, "Lord, he whom you love is ill." ⁴ But when Jesus heard it he said, "This illness does not lead to death. It is for the glory of God, so that the Son of God may be glorified through it."

⁵ Now Jesus loved Martha and her sister and Lazarus. ⁶ So, when he heard that Lazarus was ill, he stayed two days longer in the place where he was. ⁷ Then after this he said to the disciples, "Let us go to Judea again." ⁸ The disciples said to him, "Rabbi, the Jews were just now seeking to stone you, and are you going there again?" ⁹ Jesus answered, "Are there not twelve hours in the day? If anyone walks in the day, he does not stumble, because he sees the light of this world. ¹⁰ But if anyone walks in the night, he stumbles, because the light is not in him." ¹¹ After saying these things, he said to them, "Our friend Lazarus has fallen asleep, but I go to awaken him." ¹² The disciples said to him, "Lord, if he has fallen asleep, he will recover." ¹³ Now Jesus had spoken of his death, but they thought that he meant taking rest in sleep. ¹⁴ Then Jesus

told them plainly, "Lazarus has died, [15] and for your sake I am glad that I was not there, so that you may believe. But let us go to him." [16] So Thomas, called the Twin, said to his fellow disciples, "Let us also go, that we may die with him."

[17] Now when Jesus came, he found that Lazarus had already been in the tomb four days. [18] Bethany was near Jerusalem, about two miles off, [19] and many of the Jews had come to Martha and Mary to console them concerning their brother. [20] So when Martha heard that Jesus was coming, she went and met him, but Mary remained seated in the house. [21] Martha said to Jesus, "Lord, if you had been here, my brother would not have died. [22] But even now I know that whatever you ask from God, God will give you." [23] Jesus said to her, "Your brother will rise again." [24] Martha said to him, "I know that he will rise again in the resurrection on the last day." [25] Jesus said to her, "I am the resurrection and the life. Whoever believes in me, though he die, yet shall he live, [26] and everyone who lives and believes in me shall never die. Do you believe this?" [27] She said to him, "Yes, Lord; I believe that you are the Christ, the Son of God, who is coming into the world."

[28] When she had said this, she went and called her sister Mary, saying in private, "The Teacher is here and is calling for you." [29] And when she heard it, she rose quickly and went to him. [30] Now Jesus had not yet come into the village, but was still in the place where Martha had met him. [31] When the Jews who were with her in the house, consoling her, saw Mary rise quickly and go out,

they followed her, supposing that she was going to the tomb to weep there. ³² Now when Mary came to where Jesus was and saw him, she fell at his feet, saying to him, "Lord, if you had been here, my brother would not have died." ³³ When Jesus saw her weeping, and the Jews who had come with her also weeping, he was deeply moved in his spirit and greatly troubled. ³⁴ And he said, "Where have you laid him?" They said to him, "Lord, come and see." ³⁵ Jesus wept. ³⁶ So the Jews said, "See how he loved him!" ³⁷ But some of them said, "Could not he who opened the eyes of the blind man also have kept this man from dying?"

³⁸ Then Jesus, deeply moved again, came to the tomb. It was a cave, and a stone lay against it. ³⁹ Jesus said, "Take away the stone." Martha, the sister of the dead man, said to him, "Lord, by this time there will be an odor, for he has been dead four days." ⁴⁰ Jesus said to her, "Did I not tell you that if you believed you would see the glory of God?" ⁴¹ So they took away the stone. And Jesus lifted up his eyes and said, "Father, I thank you that you have heard me. ⁴² I knew that you always hear me, but I said this on account of the people standing around, that they may believe that you sent me." ⁴³ When he had said these things, he cried out with a loud voice, "Lazarus, come out." ⁴⁴ The man who had died came out, his hands and feet bound with linen strips, and his face wrapped with a cloth. Jesus said to them, "Unbind him, and let him go."

⁴⁵ Many of the Jews therefore, who had come with Mary and had seen what he did, believed in him, ⁴⁶ but

some of them went to the Pharisees and told them what Jesus had done. [47] So the chief priests and the Pharisees gathered the council and said, "What are we to do? For this man performs many signs. [48] If we let him go on like this, everyone will believe in him, and the Romans will come and take away both our place and our nation." [49] But one of them, Caiaphas, who was high priest that year, said to them, "You know nothing at all. [50] Nor do you understand that it is better for you that one man should die for the people, not that the whole nation should perish." [51] He did not say this of his own accord, but being high priest that year he prophesied that Jesus would die for the nation, [52] and not for the nation only, but also to gather into one the children of God who are scattered abroad. [53] So from that day on they made plans to put him to death.

[54] Jesus therefore no longer walked openly among the Jews, but went from there to the region near the wilderness, to a town called Ephraim, and there he stayed with the disciples.

[55] Now the Passover of the Jews was at hand, and many went up from the country to Jerusalem before the Passover to purify themselves. [56] They were looking for Jesus and saying to one another as they stood in the temple, "What do you think? That he will not come to the feast at all?" [57] Now the chief priests and the Pharisees had given orders that if anyone knew where he was, he should let them know, so that they might arrest him.

JOHN 12:1-11

¹ Six days before the Passover, Jesus therefore came to Bethany, where Lazarus was, whom Jesus had raised from the dead. ² So they gave a dinner for him there. Martha served, and Lazarus was one of those reclining with him at table. ³ Mary therefore took a pound of expensive ointment made from pure nard, and anointed the feet of Jesus and wiped his feet with her hair. The house was filled with the fragrance of the perfume. ⁴ But Judas Iscariot, one of his disciples (he who was about to betray him), said, ⁵ "Why was this ointment not sold for three hundred denarii and given to the poor?" ⁶ He said this, not because he cared about the poor, but because he was a thief, and having charge of the moneybag he used to help himself to what was put into it. ⁷ Jesus said, "Leave her alone, so that she may keep it for the day of my burial. ⁸ For the poor you always have with you, but you do not always have me."

⁹ When the large crowd of the Jews learned that Jesus was there, they came, not only on account of him but also to see Lazarus, whom he had raised from the dead. ¹⁰ So the chief priests made plans to put Lazarus to death as well, ¹¹ because on account of him many of the Jews were going away and believing in Jesus.

✦ A MODERN STORY ✦

She had been paralyzed for years. It was 1922 and Mary's girlfriends were going to hear the famous healer, Smith Wigglesworth.

"Please come with us. Let him pray for you."

They begged and pleaded, but the devout Methodist didn't believe in divine healings.

"God doesn't work that way anymore," she said. "You go on without me."

But Mary's health was failing quickly. Her friends became unrelenting in their requests. They didn't want to lose young Mary.

"If we can convince him to come to the house, will you let him pray for you?"

What could it hurt to let him pray?

"Yes," Mary consented. "If he will come to the house, he may pray for me."

The young women attended the service that night and passed along their request to those in charge. The leaders of the meeting told Smith about the dying woman. He agreed to go to her after the meeting.

Night had fallen like a heavy blanket on the city streets. Mary's condition had rapidly deteriorated. The house was quiet as the young ladies entered with Smith and his friend, Mr. Fisher.

Smith and Fisher were ushered into the sickroom. The frame of the young woman was sunken into the bed. There wasn't much to be done from a medical standpoint. But Smith Wigglesworth had never gone to medical school. He was a student of the Great Physician.

He drew a vial of oil from his coat pocket and uncorked the top. Smith and Fisher prayed as they anointed Mary with oil.

Mary's chin fell to her chest and she stopped breathing. Smith pulled her from the bed and held her against the wall.

"I rebuke this death," he yelled. "In the name of Jesus, walk! In the name of Jesus, walk!"

Mary's body began to tremble from top to bottom. Smith continued to rebuke the death, and Mary's body warmed. She drew breath and walked across the room, overcoming death and the paralysis.

After her return to health Mary spoke to her doctor and others about the experience. She said she had entered the throne room of heaven. She heard singing and saw Jesus, but he motioned to her to go back through the doorway again. Then she heard Smith calling for her to walk in the name of Jesus.

Nearly thirty years later a couple in New South Wales, Australia, was reading this miraculous story. Ronald Coady and his wife were on a mission trip. They were reading Stanley Frodsham's biography of Smith Wigglesworth. They spoke about it with each other and a friend.

"Wouldn't it be something to meet that woman? What must it have been like to be brought back from death? If only we could talk to the woman."

"You know that woman," their friend replied.

"What? How could we know her?"

"She's standing right here."

Mary Pople was passing out tracts for the Coadys in New South Wales. By providence they'd found the woman who had been given new life. She was still serving God and giving him the glory.

Fifty years later another Mary would return from the dead.

Mary Neal was kayaking with her husband and friends in January 1999. It was their last day in Chile, and it was perfect. The sun was shining, a warm breeze blowing; the rapids were white and fast.

As she skimmed over the water, Mary's kayak flipped and caught between rocks. She couldn't tip it back over. She was trapped beneath the water as her husband and friends desperately tried to save her. But it wasn't enough.

It took ninety minutes to dislodge Mary and the kayak. She was pulled from the water without a pulse. No one knew for sure how long she had been dead.

Mary was brought back to earth, but not before she had a vision of heaven. She says that while she was under the water, Jesus cradled her. She was filled with peace and love—a love so absolute and pure that she could see it.

Jesus told her that she had a mission on earth and wouldn't be entering heaven just yet. Then she returned to her family and friends. She has since written two books about heaven. She gives the glory to God.[1]

✚ REFLECTION ✚

A raccoon was signaling us, lying on its back by the side of the road, one hand held straight to the sky. I wasn't sure if it was waving hello or flagging us down. I burst out laughing. My husband, who is a little more civilized than I, only smiled.

---

1   This section is based on material from the following sources:
Tim Donnelly, "5 Books and Movies That Visit Heaven and Back."
New York Post, April 8, 2014, accessed June 2018, nypost.
com/2014/04/08/5-books-and-movies-that-visit-heaven-and-back/.
Stanley Howard Frodsham, Smith Wigglesworth: Apostle of Faith
(Springfield, MO: Gospel Publishing House, 2002).
Mary Neal, "'7 Lessons from Heaven' Author Talks about
Life after Death," Today, Sept. 19, 2017, accessed June 2018,
today.com/video/-7-lessons-from-heaven-author-talks-about-life-after-
death-1049821763590.

I don't normally laugh at roadkill, but a hand-waving raccoon is funny.

I was nearly twelve when my great-grandmother died. Hers was the first death I experienced, but I knew that it was serious. Afterward came a high school friend, other grandparents, aunts and uncles, good friends, and church members. No one lives long without encountering death.

1. **What circumstances surrounded the first death you ever experienced?**

Then he said to them all: "Whoever wants to be my disciple must deny themselves and take up their cross daily and follow me. For whoever wants to save their life will lose it, but whoever loses their life for me will save it." (Luke 9:23-24 NIV)

I have been crucified with Christ and I no longer live, but Christ lives in me. The life I now live in the body, I live by faith in the Son of God, who loved me and gave himself for me. (Galatians 2:20 NIV)

I have found more than twenty references in the New Testament that either imply or outright state that I am to die to myself. Christ is to live in me and through me. And this is for the glory of God. It is an important aspect of Christianity.

2. **In what ways have you experienced your own death in order that Christ might live?**

Thomas did not lightly offer to die with Jesus. He believed it when he said they would die in Jerusalem. Martha did not give lip service to the rabbi; she knew there would be a future resurrection. Mary was heartbroken at the death of her brother. She knew Jesus could have done something to help, but he was too late.

Jesus was the only one who could see that death was the answer to the problem.

3. Have you ever found death to be the answer to the problem? If so, why?

If the disciples were going to follow him, they had to follow wholeheartedly. For nearly all of them it resulted in death: torturous, untimely, horrific death. Except for John, church tradition names all the apostles as martyrs for Christ.

Martha saw a possible solution to death, but it was far removed from her present reality. Her brother, perhaps her only source of income and protection, was gone. She believed in a future solution that did nothing for her right then.

Mary viewed death as final. There had been hope, but now there wasn't. The one with power to do something hadn't been there when he was needed most.

Jesus met each of them where they were. It wasn't time for his death yet, he told the disciples. "Yes, there is a future, but there is also a present," he assured Martha. "Show me what you think is insurmountable," he commanded Mary.

Not everyone gets to be raised from the dead. Jesus said the resurrection of Lazarus was to bring glory to God, not to end the pain and suffering of his sisters. Eventually Lazarus died again; in fact he made it less than a week before his next death was being planned.

Death isn't the issue. Bringing glory to God is the point.

Jesus came to suffer, not because he was some masochistic god, but because his resurrection would reflect the Father's love, mercy, and forgiveness. Lazarus's resurrection showed Jesus's power over death. Smith Wigglesworth healed thousands of people and raised several to life, but he never claimed to have done it himself. He always gave credit to Jesus.

4. **Do you believe that people overcome death today in the name of Jesus? Why or why not?**

Do an internet search for "recent people come back to life" and you'll get hits from CNN, personal blogs, international newspapers, Christian magazines, and Hebrew universities. People write books about their experiences. Doctors scratch their heads.

There are many stories of people returning to life on the surgery table, the ambulance gurney, the battlefield, and at auto accidents. We don't know why some people die and don't return, and why others do come back to tell about it. Some of them turn their new lives over to God; others do not.

We all know people who suffer for years and then die, yet even in death they remind us of God. An ALS victim struggles to breathe but blows the Spirit on all she encounters. The cancer victim loses her hair and her energy but never her love of people. The dementia patient can't remember your name, but he never forgets to praise the Father's. And even in their deaths we glorify God for their grace and the peace they brought us.

So many of us wish that our loved ones would come back to life, but to return to this life is to return to the same old problems. The father with heart disease will still have a fragile heart. The aunt with kidney disease will still need dialysis.

The child with a failing marriage will still have arguments and inconsistencies.

5. **Would things be different if Jesus stepped in and saved/resurrected your loved one from death?**

Jesus offers resurrection in this life to some, but to everyone he offers re-creation. He can help change a life of fear to one of boldness. He offers peace to the anxious. He fills the hateful with love, the downhearted with joy, and the wandering with purpose.

What will you do with your new life? Will you use it to glorify God?

Perhaps you aren't facing death or suffering, but you are experiencing a blessing. What are you doing in the blessing that glorifies the Father?

Can you stand with Jesus and say, "I knew that you always hear me, but I said this for the benefit of the people standing here, that they may believe that you sent me" (John 11:42 NIV)?

6. **Make a commitment now, if you can, to resurrect your body to a life of service to God. What will be your first three steps on this new path?**

✦ ACTION ✦

1. Don't let death capture its prey. Share stories of those who have gone before. How did your grandmother bring glory to God? Why do you remember that old man in the fourth row at church? How did your friend stay faithful to God in the face of great pain and hardship? Share your stories over a cup of coffee,

on social media, or over the phone. Don't let anything stop you.

2. Who among your friends died in the past year? Who among your friends lost someone to death this past year? Tell your friends and family what you loved about the deceased. Call or send a card, a letter, or an email. Knowing that others remember the good things their loved ones did will encourage them and bring glory to God at the same time.

3. Don't wait for death. Experience resurrection today. Ask God to bring life and light into your very being. Look for ways you can be the hands and feet of Christ. Make a commitment to devote your life to Christ. Ask people in your group to share any insight for your calling that they may have.

CHAPTER 9

HE IS

✠ A REUNION ✠

Caleb nestled his face deeper into his father's neck. The gray light creeping among the trees cast shadows on the faces around him. Paul stood at his father's side, his head resting near Caleb's foot. Caleb nudged Paul's head with his toe, and his mother moved between them.

"Look up. It's time to say good-bye," Caleb's father said, jostling the boy against his chest.

Caleb saw John near the coals of last night's fire.

"Will we ride home on the same ship?" Caleb asked.

"Yes."

A circle of quiet adults and sleepy children was forming. A few of the women hugged each other, then wiped their tears.

"My children," John said as he joined the circle. "I was blessed this week by your stories. Your lives are candles dipping in the firelight, touching other candles, lanterns, and even larger fires.

Now it's time to carry your lights back to the others. The night cannot stand against you."

Caleb yawned and wrapped his arms tighter around his father's neck.

"Stand beside me," his father whispered as he placed Caleb on the opposite side of Paul.

"Your lives and the lives of those whom Jesus touched are important," John went on. "You've shared your stories with each other, showing that Jesus was the Christ, but these are just the beginning. I cannot even begin to tell you all of the signs Jesus performed while I walked with him."

John stopped to look around the circle. He motioned to Caleb and said, "Come here."

Caleb looked up at his father.

Papa smiled and gently pushed Caleb's back. "Go on."

Caleb walked to the old man. John grasped Caleb's shoulders and turned him round to face the circle.

"There was one sign that shone its light on every one of you, and its light continues to break through the darkness. It was on a morning like this."

Everyone nodded. A few looked at each other and smiled.

"You must continue to tell that story. Tell it to your children. Tell it to your neighbors. Tell it to your slaves and your masters. Tell it until every person on earth knows the story. It's the most important story." John squeezed Caleb's shoulders. "So that these children may walk in the light."

John bowed his head and prayed. The group of travelers stood shoulder to shoulder as the sun came over the horizon.

"Go in peace," John said as he lifted his face to the warm glow.

The travelers broke into smaller groups. Some headed east; several went south toward the port.

Caleb held his father's hand as they passed under the trees. "Do you know the morning story?" Caleb asked.

His father looked down at him, his eyebrows gathered in a question. "The 'Morning Story'?"

"John said everyone knows it. I don't know it." Caleb raised his shoulders in confusion.

"Ahh." His father nodded. "I know the morning story very well. That's my story."

"Your story?" Paul asked, grabbing his father's other hand.

"Yes. My mother—your Grandmother Mary—was Jesus's friend. She was tormented by demons for many years, but Jesus cast them out of her, and she never left his side after that. She was there for the miracles, and the feasts, and the teaching. And she was there for the crucifixion."

His voice grew quiet.

"I already knew that," Paul said, looking at Caleb.

"But why is it a morning story?" Caleb asked, pulling on his father's hand.

"After they killed Jesus, he was placed in a tomb. It was Passover. You remember Passover from last year, right?"

Caleb nodded.

"Everyone had to go back to their houses and rest for the Sabbath. My mother wanted to honor Jesus, to say thank you one last time. As soon as the Sabbath was over, she went to the tomb to prepare his body with spices. But when she got there, she couldn't find Jesus."

"She got lost?" Caleb asked.

"No." His father laughed. "She knew where the tomb was, but Jesus wasn't there. The sun was just coming up. The large stone in front of the tomb had been rolled away. Mother looked inside, but there wasn't a body in the grave. It scared her so badly, she ran back to the other disciples."

"Oh." Caleb nodded. "But where was Jesus?"

"I'm getting to it." His father smiled down at him. "Peter and John ran to the tomb. John was fast, and he got there first."

"Really?" Caleb's eyes grew round.

"Well, John was much younger then." He chuckled and shook the boy's hand clasped in his own. "Anyway, John and Peter got to the tomb and found it just like Mother had said. Jesus was gone. They saw the death cloths that had been wrapped around Jesus's body, but they were all rolled up neatly in the corner. There wasn't a body anywhere."

"I don't like ghost stories, not even in the morning," Caleb said.

He grasped his father's hand more tightly and walked a little closer to him.

"But it isn't a ghost story. Just wait." He took a deep breath and looked up at the trees. The light had turned from gray to golden pink. "Mother—Grandmother Mary— had followed Peter and John back to the tomb. When they didn't find anyone there, Peter and John went back home. But my mother stayed. She was crying just outside the tomb."

"Did Grandmother cry a lot?"

"I imagine she did. Jesus was her best friend and she loved him like a brother."

"Mm," Caleb said.

He and Paul looked at each other.

"After a while she dried her eyes a little and looked back in the tomb. I guess she thought maybe she was mistaken. Then what do you suppose she saw?"

"Jesus!" Caleb shouted.

"No. She saw two angels, dressed in white and shining like the sun."

Caleb's pink lips formed a perfect circle of surprise. "Oh."

"But she didn't know they were angels; she was so upset by everything. The angels asked her why she was crying, and she said that she was looking for Jesus. Then a man came up behind her and asked who she was looking for.

"Mother was so distraught, she started crying harder and told the man she couldn't find Jesus. She thought the stranger must be the gardener, so she asked him where Jesus had been taken. Then the man spoke Mother's name, and she looked at him for the first time. Do you know who it was?"

"Jesus?!" Caleb skipped a few steps.

"Yes." His father smiled. "It was Jesus. He was alive, and it was the third day since his death. He told Grandmother Mary to go tell everyone that he wasn't dead and that he would come see them soon. So Grandmother Mary was the first one to ever tell the Morning Story."

"Tell it again!"

Caleb skipped in front of his father. He grabbed the little boy and threw him on his shoulders.

"Forever and ever, as many times as you wish," he said.

✠ AN ANCIENT STORY ✠
(JOHN 19:28-42 – 20)

After the healing of the man born blind in chapter 10, Jesus said that he had the authority to lay down his life and to take it up again. In 19:30, John tells us that Jesus used that authority and "gave up his spirit." Other translations use "delivered" his spirit. Think of it as handing over his spirit.

He had been handed over to the chief priests and Pharisees. He was handed over to Herod and Pilate. He was handed over to the soldiers for flogging and crucifixion. But now it was Jesus who would do the final handing over.

1. **What do you imagine Jesus was thinking as he handed his life over for you?**

John tells us it was Preparation Day when Jesus was crucified. Preparation Day was when the Passover lambs were slaughtered to prepare for Passover the next day. Because that year Passover would begin on the Sabbath, it would be a special event.

The Jewish leaders didn't want to contaminate the land by leaving dead bodies on the crosses. The country had to be clean and pure for the Passover. If dying bodies were left on the crosses, animals might come to eat the bodies. Carrion would be dragged across the land and Passover would be desecrated.

The leaders wanted to be saved by the rules while the Ruler was there saving them.

2. **Are there any rules you feel you must follow to keep Jesus and his Father happy?**

This was the darkest, most dangerous time for the disciples of Jesus thus far. Their leader had been taken away, beaten, and crucified. They weren't sure what was going to happen, but they knew they were likely to be next. Yet John stayed until the very end by the cross. Perhaps he stayed with Mary and the other women (Matthew 27:56, Mark 15:40, Luke 23:49) to offer protection and comfort, but I think he stayed because he loved Jesus. Whatever the reason, staying around would have been ill-advised.

Then Joseph of Arimathea asked Pilate for the body and placed it in his own family tomb. This was remarkable for many reasons. First, Jesus had been crucified for treason. He'd claimed to be a king. Other executed criminals could have been buried by relatives or friends, but treason was such an odious crime that the offenders were not allowed this familial compassion.

Second, Joseph was a member of the Sanhedrin. Asking for the body of Jesus meant that he would no longer be a secret disciple. There would be no going back, no defense. He would be cut off from all power and prestige. He was giving up his way of life.

Third, a tomb was expensive real estate. It was an investment in your family, your finances, and your faith. The scriptures say this was a new tomb for Joseph. He was born in Arimathea, a small village probably in the hill country of Ephraim, far from Jerusalem. Matthew's gospel tells us that Joseph was rich, and Mark and Luke's gospels say he was a man of importance. So he appeared to be a man who had moved up in the world and made a name for himself. The purchase of a tomb in Jerusalem was probably the final rung on the ladder of success. Now he was throwing it all away.

But Joseph didn't act alone. Nicodemus finally made a decision as well. He joined Joseph in the extravagant display of love and devotion by bringing the spices for the burial. The large amount of spices used was indicative of their belief that Jesus had been an intended king.

I stress this section of John because it is important to remember that at this point neither the disciples, the women, Joseph, nor Nicodemus expected a resurrection. They'd taken a stand for what was right, even to the peril of their own lives. They stood up in the middle of darkness and shined their light.

3.   What would you have done? What are you doing?

Mary Magdalene loved Jesus; there can be no doubt. When the disciples were hiding in their homes, she was searching for Jesus's body. After the disciples returned home, understanding that some miracle had occurred, Mary still cried in the garden. She stayed with the tomb like a dog stays near its master even in death.

When Jesus made himself known to Mary, she fell in worship and held to his feet. Jesus told her she mustn't cling to him.

She couldn't take control of Jesus. She had to give herself over to him.

4.   Have you ever tried to manipulate or control Jesus? What did you learn?

In 20:17, Jesus directed Mary to share the news of the resurrection. He told her to go to his "brothers"—not his "disciples," not his "servants," not even his "friends." They were now his brothers.

Do you notice a repetitive phrase in 20:19-29? "Peace be with you." It was a common belief that to see God was to be in imminent danger of judgment. In Judges 6, for example, Gideon saw an angel of the Lord and believed he was going to die. The disciples had witnessed signs and miracles for several years. They saw Jesus take control of earth's forces. They saw him wither a tree, calm the wind and waves, and heal diseases. He even had control over spiritual realms by commanding demons to leave. Peter, James, and John had witnessed the transfiguration of Jesus with Moses and Elijah.

But this was the first time that Jesus had to say, "Peace be with you." It is obvious that something supernatural had occurred without precedence or expectation.

This was the final sign. Jesus was and forever is the Messiah.

JOHN 19:28-42

28 After this, Jesus, knowing that all was now finished, said (to fulfill the Scripture), "I thirst." 29 A jar full of sour wine stood there, so they put a sponge full of the sour wine on a hyssop branch and held it to his mouth. 30 When Jesus had received the sour wine, he said, "It is finished," and he bowed his head and gave up his spirit.

31 Since it was the day of Preparation, and so that the bodies would not remain on the cross on the Sabbath (for that Sabbath was a high day), the Jews asked Pilate that their legs might be broken and that they might be taken away. 32 So the soldiers came and broke the legs of the first, and of the other who had been crucified with him. 33 But when they came to Jesus and saw that he was already

dead, they did not break his legs. [34] But one of the soldiers pierced his side with a spear, and at once there came out blood and water. [35] He who saw it has borne witness—his testimony is true, and he knows that he is telling the truth—that you also may believe. [36] For these things took place that the Scripture might be fulfilled: "Not one of his bones will be broken." [37] And again another Scripture says, "They will look on him whom they have pierced."

[38] After these things Joseph of Arimathea, who was a disciple of Jesus, but secretly for fear of the Jews, asked Pilate that he might take away the body of Jesus, and Pilate gave him permission. So he came and took away his body. [39] Nicodemus also, who earlier had come to Jesus by night, came bringing a mixture of myrrh and aloes, about seventy-five pounds in weight. [40] So they took the body of Jesus and bound it in linen cloths with the spices, as is the burial custom of the Jews. [41] Now in the place where he was crucified there was a garden, and in the garden a new tomb in which no one had yet been laid. [42] So because of the Jewish day of Preparation, since the tomb was close at hand, they laid Jesus there.

JOHN 20

[1] Now on the first day of the week Mary Magdalene came to the tomb early, while it was still dark, and saw that the stone had been taken away from the tomb. [2] So she ran and went to Simon Peter and the other disciple, the one whom Jesus loved, and said to them, "They have taken

the Lord out of the tomb, and we do not know where they have laid him." ³ So Peter went out with the other disciple, and they were going toward the tomb. ⁴ Both of them were running together, but the other disciple outran Peter and reached the tomb first. ⁵ And stooping to look in, he saw the linen cloths lying there, but he did not go in. ⁶ Then Simon Peter came, following him, and went into the tomb. He saw the linen cloths lying there, ⁷ and the face cloth, which had been on Jesus' head, not lying with the linen cloths but folded up in a place by itself. ⁸ Then the other disciple, who had reached the tomb first, also went in, and he saw and believed; ⁹ for as yet they did not understand the Scripture, that he must rise from the dead. ¹⁰ Then the disciples went back to their homes.

¹¹ But Mary stood weeping outside the tomb, and as she wept she stooped to look into the tomb. ¹² And she saw two angels in white, sitting where the body of Jesus had lain, one at the head and one at the feet. ¹³ They said to her, "Woman, why are you weeping?" She said to them, "They have taken away my Lord, and I do not know where they have laid him." ¹⁴ Having said this, she turned around and saw Jesus standing, but she did not know that it was Jesus. ¹⁵ Jesus said to her, "Woman, why are you weeping? Whom are you seeking?" Supposing him to be the gardener, she said to him, "Sir, if you have carried him away, tell me where you have laid him, and I will take him away." ¹⁶ Jesus said to her, "Mary." She turned and said to him in Aramaic, "Rabboni!" (which means Teacher). ¹⁷ Jesus said to her, "Do not cling to me, for I have not yet ascended to the Father; but go to my

brothers and say to them, 'I am ascending to my Father and your Father, to my God and your God.'" [18] Mary Magdalene went and announced to the disciples, "I have seen the Lord"—and that he had said these things to her.

[19] On the evening of that day, the first day of the week, the doors being locked where the disciples were for fear of the Jews, Jesus came and stood among them and said to them, "Peace be with you." [20] When he had said this, he showed them his hands and his side. Then the disciples were glad when they saw the Lord. [21] Jesus said to them again, "Peace be with you. As the Father has sent me, even so I am sending you." [22] And when he had said this, he breathed on them and said to them, "Receive the Holy Spirit. [23] If you forgive the sins of any, they are forgiven them; if you withhold forgiveness from any, it is withheld."

[24] Now Thomas, one of the twelve, called the Twin, was not with them when Jesus came. [25] So the other disciples told him, "We have seen the Lord." But he said to them, "Unless I see in his hands the mark of the nails, and place my finger into the mark of the nails, and place my hand into his side, I will never believe."

[26] Eight days later, his disciples were inside again, and Thomas was with them. Although the doors were locked, Jesus came and stood among them and said, "Peace be with you." [27] Then he said to Thomas, "Put your finger here, and see my hands; and put out your hand, and place it in my side. Do not disbelieve, but believe." [28] Thomas answered him, "My Lord and my God!" [29] Jesus said to him, "Have you believed because you have seen me? Blessed are those who have not seen and yet have believed."

[30] Now Jesus did many other signs in the presence of the disciples, which are not written in this book; [31] but these are written so that you may believe that Jesus is the Christ, the Son of God, and that by believing you may have life in his name.

✤ A MODERN STORY ✤

There is no modern savior. God hasn't sent his second son, or his daughter, nephew, cousin, or aunt. There isn't any need. But resurrection stories abound.

There is resurrection when a prodigal daughter calls home to ask if she can return. No questions are asked. No accusations lobbed across the living room. Hugs and kisses and a whole lot of faith bring the dead child back to life.

Resurrection happens when neighbors whose families have hated each other for generations decide to clear the air. Hateful words are forgiven as the two families laugh together over a shared meal. Their new relationship brings hope for a better future.

And resurrection occurs when a husband turns his back on his own grief and pain and forgives his adulterous wife. They renew their vows, recommit to caring for each other. And love is reborn.

The details may never get plastered all over social media, but everyone will know. The black cloud has cleared. The iron curtain has torn. The death grip of Satan has loosed in the love of Jesus.

Everyone knows because you have to tell a story like that.

I was so embarrassed. The poor man was just trying to deliver the winter gas. He wasn't there for a sermon or a lecture, but he was going to hear one whether he wanted to or not. Grandma had spotted him and headed out the door. When she returned, she was frustrated.

"What is wrong with people that they don't want to talk about God? He's God!"

My grandmother believed the Lord Jesus Christ came in the flesh, lived, suffered, died, and was raised again. She believed that this resurrection sign was intended for her and for all of those who came across her path. There was no stopping her from telling you.

She loved to sit across from me and talk about Jesus. She would pore through her Bible and ask me what I thought about various scriptures. She loved me deeply, but I never questioned whom she loved the most.

Telling the story is at the core of Christianity. John has given us seven signs that Jesus is the Messiah, signs that would have convinced people of his day. These same signs still serve to bring people to Jesus. Not everyone experiences all these signs, but the eighth sign, the resurrection, is the sign for all people.

Wissam moved to Michigan to share the story with Muslims. Jeffrey Dahmer shared the gospel with fellow inmates. My friends, Beth and Steven, shared the gospel with nurses and doctors as they waited for the Father to take their daughter home. They continue to preach the good news.

The Bakers lost a son, but they never lost their zeal for spreading the news that Jesus offers life. Demetra tells everyone she meets about the goodness of Jesus. When she was a new

Christian, she would say, "Jesus, I just need to lay you down a minute." Then she would revert to her old ways. She doesn't lay Jesus aside anymore, because she has experienced the strength and power of his resurrection.

Even after their deaths George Müller, John Paton, and Smith Wigglesworth are telling the story of Jesus, the Christ. Their books, foundations, and principles are still guiding people to the Lord.

Some people are healed of sickness or deformity. Others experience supernatural events, like tornadoes that rescue and shipwrecks that save. Some have family members brought back to life.

Everyone is part of the story. Jesus Christ's signs are still available today. He convinces the football player, the lead singer, the father, and the child. Jesus comes to the farmer, the doctor, and the preacher. He works miracles for the blind, the broken, and the demon-possessed.

His story began before time, and it is still being told.

Jesus said to her, "I am the resurrection and the life. The one who believes in me will live, even though they die; and whoever lives by believing in me will never die. Do you believe this?" (John 11:25-26 NIV)

✢ REFLECTION ✢

The first half of the book of John is often referred to as the "Book of Signs." Critics of Jesus were willing to acknowledge his power, but they wanted to denigrate its source. Some called him a magician; others said the power came from Satan, and those who were willing to admit he had power from God sometimes didn't have the nerve to admit that he himself was from God.

So John explained the signs.

The first two signs might have been construed as sleight of hand or coincidence. The first sign, changing the water to wine, convinced the disciples that Jesus was someone great. They believed that they should trust him. That story was followed by the Pharisees asking for a sign. Jesus implied that the only sign they would receive was the resurrection.

The second sign was a healing from a distance. Some might have said it was coincidence, that no one could heal from so far away. But the royal official and his whole household believed.

1. **Have you asked for signs from God but then counted them as coincidence?**

The third sign began to stretch people. The paralytic was healed instantaneously right in front of everyone. It was no illusion or coincidence. So why didn't the people believe the sign? Because it was performed on the Sabbath, the holy day, the day when work was forbidden. The Messiah would have surely known better than to heal on the Sabbath.

2. **In what ways has Jesus surprised you in your own life?**

The next two signs were stunning, showing power over the natural order of things. Jesus created food where there was none, and he controlled the winds and the waves. The common people were willing at this point to lay claim to the Messiah, but then he started teaching.

They didn't want a Messiah; they wanted a winning lottery ticket. They wanted food and clothing and political power. Jesus again talked about the resurrection: "No one can come to me unless the Father who sent me draws them, and I will raise them up at the last day" (6:44 NIV). The people began to leave him. The signs were not enough for them.

3. In what ways does Jesus make you uncomfortable?

The sixth sign should have proven Jesus's extraordinary power and that he was the Messiah. No one had ever healed a man born blind. Blindness as a cause of disease or age could have been healed with medicine or faith, but blindness "caused" by God as punishment for deep-rooted sin had never been healed.

The Pharisees were so determined that Jesus could not possibly be the Messiah that they didn't see the miracle right in front of them. They turned family members against each other; neighbors and brothers became enemies. They accused Jesus of being "demon-possessed and raving mad" (10:20 NIV). They gave credit to the wrong source.

4. To what or whom are you tempted to give credit for the signs that appear in your life?

The seventh sign should have left no doubt. Lazarus had been dead for four days. He was beyond the call of life. Everyone for miles around knew of his death. This was no illusion. No coincidence. No work of the devil. This was God.

John tells us that people did believe based on the raising of Lazarus. They even believed enough to go tell the Pharisees, whom everyone knew to be less than happy to hear good things about Jesus. But the Pharisees still refused to acknowledge that Jesus was the Messiah.

The prominent belief before Jesus came to earth was that the Messiah would rescue the Israelites from their enemies. He would be a strong military king in the same vein as David. Jesus was no military hero. He talked about walking extra miles to placate the Romans. He said to pay taxes to Caesar. He partied with lowlifes instead of rubbing elbows with the powerful and elite.

Despite all the signs that supported Jesus as the Messiah, the people just didn't want him for their Messiah. Plain and simple.

5. **In what ways is Jesus's lifestyle still an issue for people today?**

John tells us of one more sign, a sign so astounding it made believers of Pharisees, Jews, Gentiles, rich, poor, men, and women.

The resurrection was the sign that Jesus had promised from the beginning. He spoke of it to the crowds, to the Pharisees, and to his disciples. It was the sign that could not be denied and could not be ignored. Jesus raised himself from the dead. He was God.

Jesus still offers us signs. He is still speaking to the world, convincing men and women everywhere that he is the Savior. He saves from demons, disease, and even death. His resurrection is the sign that we too will overcome death.

Jesus says, "I am the bread of life" (6:35), but we want bread in our pockets and bread in our banks. Jesus says to look upon him, "the light of the world" (8:12), but instead we stare at the glow of backlit blue screens. Jesus proclaims that he is "the door" (10:9) and has swung it wide open, but we walk by toward another house. Jesus says he is "the vine" (15:5) and that we can be a part of him, but instead we search for inner strength and truth. Jesus states that he is "the good shepherd," (10:11) and the sheep will know his voice, but we fill our lives with so much noise that we can't hear his quiet calls. Jesus says he is "the way, and the truth, and the life" (14:6), but we choose to make our own way, determine our own truth, and define our own life.

The one sign and the one statement we should not ignore is Jesus's claim that he is "the resurrection and the life" (11:25).

Like the ancient people of Israel, so many of us just don't want to see what is right in front of us. The signs that are more than enough, are still not enough for many of us.

6. **Are they enough for you?**

✤ ACTION ✤

1. Make a list of all the signs you have witnessed that Jesus is the Christ, the Messiah. You may want to categorize them according to John's signs—supernatural, healing, overcoming death—or you may want to list them chronologically, spatially, or haphazardly. After you make your list, share it with others. Remember to tell the story to anyone who will listen.

2. Meditate on the signs of the Messiah in John. Ask God to show you where your disbelief is keeping you from following Jesus completely. Spend time in prayer confessing your disbelief and asking God for courage to believe and proclaim that Jesus is the Messiah.

3. Join in a sunrise service with your study group or several friends. Begin before dawn. Spend the dark time praying for those who haven't seen Jesus as the Christ, for those who live in darkness and despair. As the light penetrates the darkness and day dawns, worship Jesus, the light of the world.

A NOTE FROM THE AUTHOR

Paul and Caleb are conglomerations of children from my own life. I love the innocence that children display by accepting Jesus at face value.

The rest of us—the grown-ups with reason and sensibilities—are harder to convince.

John knew that. And he gave what he believed were irrefutable signs of the Christ's legitimacy.

But that was then. How can we be sure those things ever happened?

Believe me, I sometimes have doubts. I wonder how it could all be true while my friend's daughter lies in a hospital with her heart stitched back together. I see news stories on the internet and speculate how a loving God and Savior could allow such hatred and violence. I feel the anguish of a young man suffering from autism and depression, and I ask, Where is the love in that, Jesus?

And then I see the signs. The power. The changed life. The glory of God. And I just know.

Jesus was and is and forever will be the Messiah. Our Savior.

Because he still gives us signs.

MORE BOOKS BY TRACI STEAD

DEVOTIONS OF A GERBIL

God scoops us into His arms and carries us home from the shelter, but we dig holes and crawl back into the world. God whistles from His porch even while we chase cars and cats and go through the neighbors' trash.

THE SPIRIT SERIES:
THE POTTER OF PARADOX

Journey back to the first century as three siblings search for the purpose of life. Then join a modern potter as he seeks the same thing.

THE DOCTOR OF DUNSTABLE PLAINS

Why is there suffering? Will your faith survive when your prayers go unanswered? Explore these questions through the lives of an ancient doctor and a rural New Hampshire physician.

THE SHEPHERD OF SHOTTON CROSS

What do you do when right is called wrong? It's an ancient question posed by Amos the prophet and a WW1 Welsh shepherd. Does one voice really make a difference?